THE CRITICAL CORE

THE CRITICAL CORE

Eight strategy practices that give winning companies their edge

Tony Manning

PENGUIN BOOKS

Published by Penguin Books
an imprint of Penguin Random House South Africa (Pty) Ltd
Reg. No. 1953/000441/07
The Estuaries No. 4, Oxbow Crescent, Century Avenue, Century City, 7441
PO Box 1144, Cape Town, 8000, South Africa
www.penguinrandomhouse.co.za

Penguin Random House South Africa

First published 2017

1 3 5 7 9 10 8 6 4 2

PUBLISHER: Marlene Fryer
MANAGING EDITOR: Robert Plummer
PROOFREADER: Lisa Compton
COVER AND TEXT DESIGNER: Ryan Africa
TYPESETTER: Monique van den Berg

Set in 10.5 pt on 15 pt Minion

solutions
Printed by **novus print**, a Novus Holdings company

MIX
Paper from responsible sources
FSC® C022948
FSC www.fsc.org

This book is printed on FSC® certified and controlled sources. FSC (Forest Stewardship Council®) is an independent, international, non-governmental organization. Its aim is to support environmentally sustainable, socially and economically responsible global forest management.

ISBN 978 1 77609 188 1 (print)
ISBN 978 1 77609 189 8 (ePub)

CONTENTS

INTRODUCTION

WHY THIS BOOK?

Why do we make management so damned hard?

This question has perplexed me for years, and it's one that should bother every executive. Running any business is a challenge. Easy days are few and far between. There's always another surprise, another issue screaming for attention, another reason to take your eye off your plans and reach for the nearest quick fix. And amid all this, results are all too often held hostage to action lists that keep getting longer, to unaligned and demotivated employees – and, worst of all, to a barrage of fads and flaky ideas which supposedly will make things better, but in fact just make them worse.

Your goal should be to make life easier, not more difficult. And this book will help you. For it describes a simple, sound, and practical approach to business leadership that's based on just one tool – *strategic conversation* – and centred on two words: *strategy* and *people*.

Strategy determines where and how you'll compete. People are the mind and the heartbeat of every activity. Strategic conversation is the purposeful and continuous organizational dialogue that determines what your firm is about and what results it gets.

This is not to pretend that there's a magical formula for success. But it does underscore the need for focus and simplicity in an incredibly complex and tumultuous world. And it's a reminder that we don't have to fumble with a wide array of levers in pursuit of performance.

Most of us are familiar with the adage "What gets measured is what gets managed." What's left unsaid, though, is that it's only what gets *talked about* that will be either measured or managed. So what you talk about, with whom, and how, is the essential aspect of everything your firm does, the way it does everything, and the results it gets.

Think productivity, quality, innovation, agility, sales, profits – or any other outcome you seek – and think about the tools you rely on to get them. Consider what makes these tools work. In every case, it's *conversation*.

As a strategy consultant, I get to see companies warts and all. My work gives me an insider's perspective of what they actually do, and what separates winners from losers. I'm used to having CEOs assure me that their companies are quite different from all others and have the best people in their industry – but are held back by *external* factors. And while there are many reasons why most businesses do less well than they could, my overriding sense is that one stands out:

They get in their own way.

If they're not as successful as they'd like to be, it's largely because of what happens *inside* their walls rather than outside.

Consumed by operational issues, they overlook or deny external threats or opportunities. Under pressure to satisfy investors, they succumb to short-termism instead of taking a long view and working steadily towards the future they want. Lacking a considered and consistent approach to strategy, they chop and change and confuse themselves with new theories and themes. Their declaration that "our people are our most important asset" is mostly just spin. They're awash in gobbledegook, and in desperate need of a dose of common sense.

In the immortal words of comic-strip character Pogo: "*We have met the enemy, and he is us.*"

For three decades I've assisted managers* in their struggles for performance amid increasing complexity and uncertainty. I've been there as they wrestled with strategy; listened to them agonise over the best way to develop it and get buy-in from their teams; and learned how hard it is to turn good plans into action. And I've been constantly astounded by the zeal with which so many of them skip from fad to fad, searching desperately for some "silver bullet" that might give them an extra edge.

Along the way, I've spent countless hours studying virtually every aspect of management, and using this knowledge in my work with clients, in the numerous books and articles I've written, in business school lectures, and in speeches. So I've been able to combine tried-and-true concepts and the latest ideas with lessons from the school of hard knocks, and to look at what management thinkers say through the lens of what practising managers do.

At first, not surprisingly, I learned a great deal. But it wasn't long before I noticed that a few ideas were cropping up again and again. In different contexts and guises, to be sure – packaged and promoted under different names, promising new benefits, explained in new ways, enriched with new examples, and bolstered by new data – but there they were, a handful of them that ran through many decades and often across disciplines.

There were marketing insights, for example, that applied equally to strategy. Thoughts on strategy infused the leadership literature. Leadership know-how was an essential factor in change management. People issues were central to quality, innovation,

* Throughout this book, I use the terms *managers*, *leaders*, and *executives* interchangeably, as they all have the same role: to get results through other people.

and lean production – and, of course, to agility and resilience. And so on.

As I looked back across 100 years of management thought, or dug into new stuff that looked promising, and asked, "*What is the underlying message?*" and "*How is this new?*" it mostly turned out to be just a repeat. This was always a let-down, but I came to expect it. On the other hand, the fact that the same few ideas kept being reaffirmed, from this angle and that, along with fresh evidence of their value, evidently meant that they mattered to both management thinking and management *practice* – and thus to business performance.

And so it was that I came to a troubling paradox ... and *within it* a blindingly obvious way to get the results we want.

The paradox is this:

> *Over the past century or so, the management advice industry – whose purpose, you'd think, is to help managers improve their performance – has churned out more concepts, theories, methods, models, frameworks, and questionnaires than any executive can ever use.*[1] *And they keep coming. Yet efforts to push forward the boundaries of management thought and practice have been largely futile.*

I've thought long and hard about this assertion, because it's a contentious one and sure to draw flak. I have no wish to play down the importance of management ideas, or take potshots at well-intended efforts to advance management thinking. I'm all in favour of finding better ways to manage.

But there's no getting away from these six facts:

1. Business is the engine of society, and will fund or otherwise facilitate most of the progress we need. So the future of human-

kind depends on managerial performance – and that performance overall is disappointing.

2. Most companies do not achieve even average results, and certainly not with any consistency. Their life expectancy is falling. Their financial returns have flattened or declined. And since future global economic growth is likely to be slower than in the past, leading to increasingly vicious competition, better sales and profits will be increasingly hard to come by.
3. Managers are overloaded with advice, much of which is clearly failing them. There are many ways to do things, but the use of just about any management tool is *arbitrary* – and there's no evident downside to *not* using most of them.
4. Hype about "reinventing management" has not translated into reality. Most changes in management practice over the past 100 years have come in response to social, technological, or other *contextual* shifts. Not only has a small set of basics endured, but most seemingly "new" ideas are actually just more of the same.
5. Although yet-to-be-discovered management ideas may have some impact on business performance, no one knows when to expect them or can sit around doing nothing while waiting. Meanwhile, failure to excel in *known* practices will ensure that firms do not exploit opportunities that exist all around them, and that profits keep falling through the cracks.

Finally – and this is the one that should bother us the most:

6. The most vocal critics of management scholars' research methods, the relevance and practical value of their outputs, their inability to add much that's new to management thinking, and the course offerings and teaching methods of business schools

are *insiders*, not *outsiders*. They include some of the world's most respected management professors and a growing number of business school deans.

You could read the paradox as negative:

We're in trouble because management thinking is out of gas.

But it has a positive side too:

New management ideas might be few and far between, but fortunately there's less to making a business competitive than you might think. We already know what matters, what works, what we have to do. And since most firms don't do it, do only some of it, or do it badly, the way is open for you to gain the advantage you want faster and more easily than you might dare hope.

The answer lies in a small set of practices that show up repeatedly, meet a set of rigorous criteria, and are necessary in all companies, in all industries, across the world.

There are eight of them. They're so essential to business performance that it's appropriate to call them *"the critical core."*

These practices are not add-ons or options you can elect to use or not use on a whim.

They are what all managers *must do.*

They are what you and your team *must do.*

This, then, was the theme of my previous book *What's Wrong With Management and How to Get It Right* (published by Penguin in 2015). From the time I began writing it, I grappled with how to strike the best balance between laying out the evidence for my views, and explaining the critical core. In the end, because nobody else had made the same argument in the same way, and it is such a serious one, I gave eight chapters to the evidence and just three to the practices.

After the book was published, I got excellent feedback from many senior executives, along with numerous requests for a shorter version that dealt specifically with the eight practices. They wanted the "how-to" material to be more accessible.

The Critical Core answers that call.

Readers of *What's Wrong With Management* will find themselves on familiar ground here. But although I've naturally used a good deal of material that appeared previously, I've clarified some issues, elaborated on the practices, and added advice where necessary.

As was the case with *What's Wrong With Management*, this book doesn't promise yet another "groundbreaking" theory, tool, or technique. There are no quick fixes here. No buzzwords or snappy slogans. Instead, I reiterate why you *don't* need any of those; why you should instead get back to a few critical strategy practices that are well known; and why they offer you the best chance of getting the results you want.

Once again, I contend that there's compelling proof that the way to build your competitive advantage, capture and keep customers, and stay ahead in the profit game lies in what you may already know but just aren't focusing on. And that if you want to be a serious competitor today and tomorrow, less really is more and simpler is better.

One thing you'll notice in these pages is my frequent references to Peter Drucker. I make no apologies for this, since he's an invaluable resource. Not for nothing is he called "the father of modern management" – or, as Warren Bennis put it, "the most important management thinker of our time."[2]

Almost anything worth saying about the subject today was first said by him – and usually said better than by anyone else. I cite him not only because of his insights, but because tracing the roots of various "new" ideas to him underscores just how few of them really are new.

The Critical Core will help you unclutter your toolkit, develop a clear point of view about how to take your firm into the future, and manage it in the way most likely to bring success. It will also help you put whatever new ideas you come across into perspective, and evaluate them sensibly before you try them – perhaps at great cost and with unhelpful consequences.

The practices are *what* you must do. *How* you apply each of them depends not only on skill, but also on a variety of insights, concepts, or techniques. There's a shedload of these, and there will be even more in the future, for this is where most study, development, and promotion – so-called thought leadership – occurs. But I urge you to treat whatever you come across with caution, and keep your toolkit as light as you can. Begin with the advice I offer here, give it your all, and resist the temptation to dabble with other ideas until you're absolutely sure you need them.

This is bound to be a challenge that will test your resolve. New tools will keep coming and the hype around them will be mind-numbing. It will no doubt suit their vendors to make them as complex as possible, to persuade you that their help is essential in applying them, and to stretch their involvement for as long as they can – after all, this is how they make a living. So you're unlikely to hear them say, "This is really simple; let's spend a day talking about what you need to know, and you and your team can get moving."

But I *want* you to know just how simple it is.

And how easily you can get going.

And I want to help you embrace and exploit these truths:

1. Winners do a few very basic things, very well, that losers don't do.
2. What you've been doing to take you forward has probably held you back.
3. Your company is most likely to be successful if you get back to the principal drivers of business results – what you absolutely must obsess about – and then apply them in the simplest, most practical way possible.

Leading any company in this fractious and fast-moving world is complicated work. The pressures are extraordinary.

You have to move fast. You have to keep innovating and improving. You have to enlist the imagination and spirit of all your people in your quest to be competitive.

But first, you have to free up time to think.

None of this is possible while you keep cluttering your organization with conceptual junk, confusing your team with buzzwords, or encumbering them with methods that supposedly will lead to better results, but in fact just keep them from productive work.

The Critical Core will take only a couple of hours to read. It'll save you a lifetime of searching for more complicated and costly answers.

1

GETTING TO THE CORE

The most pressing management need of our time is *to know and apply the practices that make the difference between winning and losing in business.*

There's nothing new about this. But there is a special urgency now to get it right.

Following the global financial crisis of 2008, most economies are still struggling to recover, and many economists believe slow growth will continue for many years – perhaps even *decades* – into the future. Companies everywhere are struggling for sales and profits. And odds are there are tougher times ahead.

Competition is becoming ever more hostile. Massive social and political shifts are under way. The effects of global warming are becoming ever more devastating. Technological breakthroughs are disrupting industries, threatening jobs, and transforming the way we live and work.

And the challenges don't end there.

Many firms operate within complex webs of stakeholders, all hustling for influence and some becoming dangerously powerful. New regulation, social media, rising consumer power, and global supply chains all muddy the waters.

Overall, the world is in what the military calls a VUCA state – *volatile, uncertain, complex,* and *ambiguous.* Making sense of what's happening gets harder by the minute. Even seemingly minor decisions are fraught with risk.

Within this rapidly changing context, firms find themselves constantly at what Andy Grove, the former chairman of Intel, famously called "a strategic inflection point" – a moment when yesterday's strategy is threatened and a new one becomes imperative. A moment of both daunting problems and extraordinary possibilities.[1] The choices managers make in the present define their long-term prospects and performance. But they're making bets on a future they can't see and often can't even imagine.

The roles and responsibilities of companies are different today than they were in the past. Many of the challenges they face are unprecedented. They, more than any other social institution, determine our future. So troubled firms must be quickly fixed, and the strategies of those that are doing well must be fine-tuned or reinvented.

In this, your first and ongoing task as a leader – a strategist – is to frame the way you and others see the world. To craft and conduct a strategic conversation that makes sense of today's realities and shines a light on tomorrow's possibilities. To inspire a common purpose among disparate stakeholders who see things from their own perspectives, coloured by their own assumptions, experiences, values, and interests. And to define, drive, and facilitate the actions that will lead to a desired future.

Management ideas are key to this process. They're at once a language[2] and a lens. More than just a basis for *discussing* and *doing*, they also affect *seeing* and *being*. So they have a profound impact on what gets attention in any organization; what gets talked about and how; the way strategy is thought about and created; and where and how resources are applied.

Understanding the changes around you is more necessary than ever – and more difficult. A jumble of signals and noise makes it all but impossible to know what's coming next. Upheavals are normal. Growing complexity entangles every decision, and a bewildering array of factors and actors tilt outcomes one way or another. Circumstances, timing, and luck matter enormously.

All this is a given.

But when it comes to what *managers can and must do* to gain and sustain an edge, everything hinges on the critical strategy practices I mentioned earlier.

These practices give you the best possible chance of coping with whatever the world throws at you, of exploiting emerging opportunities, and of out-innovating and outrunning your competitors.

They are what the winners *do* that puts them ahead in the race for customers and profits.

Each of the eight critical strategy practices is a source of competitive strength. Together, they comprise a "strategy system" that frames strategic conversation and focuses attention on what really matters, and, as a bonus, helps you combat what is undoubtedly the most prevalent and pernicious destroyer of value – what I call "the tyranny of tools."

Some of the management tools we have are clearly valuable. Most, however, add nothing to what you need, and, if truth be told, are worth more to the experts who produce them than to the firms that fall for them. But there's so much hype, it's hard to know which to go for and which to ignore. And it's a fair bet that, like most managers, you'll try too many and inadvertently throw sand in the gears of your business.

Disruption!

Organizations are complex systems and never in a perfect state. They're always in tension between stability and chaos, repetition and renewal. It's easier to screw them up than make them hum, and managers are at the mercy of a slew of factors beyond their control. Learning how to apply any new tool, how it fits with what's there, and what effect it has always takes longer than anyone imagines, and every intervention has unanticipated consequences, good or bad.

But there's more to worry about.

As managers strive for growth in conditions that are more testing by the day, it's essential that they bring as much *stability* and *repeatability* as possible to their organizations. But it's equally essential that they keep their teams on edge, constantly alert, challenging the status quo, reinventing every aspect of what they do and how they do it, and exploring possibilities that may be fraught with risk.

As they grapple with the complexities of their business amid a hail of surprises, they have to keep questioning their own assumptions, beliefs, and values; rethinking the best way forward; adjusting their plans; shifting the deck chairs. All this is deeply unsettling to everyone, and its full impact on business performance may only be evident long after the event.

It's perplexing, then, that managers so enthusiastically amplify this disruption and turbocharge their troubles. That they waste as much time, effort, and money as they do on complicating their lives, making work more difficult than it need be, and shoving the results they want further and further out into the future.

Just as the aim of strategy must be to deal with a clearly defined challenge – either a problem or an opportunity – so should management ideas *only be adopted for a specific purpose.* Accordingly, they should be carefully evaluated and chosen, well understood, and sparingly used. They are too important to be toyed with.

Too often, though, executives settle on answers before they've clarified their questions. Under pressure to make decisions in circumstances they cannot fully comprehend, they're drawn to "solutions" they don't need and won't be able to use to best effect. Then they trigger a bullshit alert when they pepper their conversations with buzzwords, and undermine their own credibility when they trot out half-baked thoughts on "best practices," picked up from who knows where, without being able to properly explain them. And when they foist what they find onto their already stretched firms, they set themselves up for failure.

This is utter madness.

But it gets worse.

Instead of focusing on one new idea and helping their people get their heads around it, and excel in it, they quickly become excited by something else. And because new challenges keep arising, they keep grasping.

Ignoring the fact that their people are under pressure and struggling with *current* problems, let alone trying to make sense of new thinking, they keep changing priorities and generating new work. They rewrite vision and mission statements, revise goals, restructure, and reengineer. They dump projects that only yesterday were "key to our success" and announce new ones that will "bring a step change in our competitiveness" – while allowing no delay or deviation from budget. They demand "out of the box" thinking, but continue to manage in ways that kill unusual ideas. And when they get together with their colleagues in a strategy retreat, they assure them, "This is not *my* strategy; it's *our* strategy."

But "our strategy" is too often *no* strategy, because no one knows what it is. (Not even the boss!) The overall picture is a blur and the bits don't hang together. And chances are it'll be different tomorrow. And again the day after that.

This rat-tat-tat of random, unclear, and mixed messages undermines understanding, morale, and performance. It leads to any number of pointless activities, spawns complexity, creates chaos and confusion when these should be fought tooth and nail, and locks people into a toxic spiral of poor performance (Figure 1.1).

Figure 1.1

These habits are fuelled by an assortment of management gurus, including scholars, consultants, writers, and speakers. And by business schools, and the media, and almost anyone with an opinion on what makes firms tick.

There's no shortage of people keen to grab your attention and tell you how to run your business. And who in their right mind would want to pass up a chance at some miracle fix? After all, if you try enough new stuff, you just might hit on what you need!

The problem is, every management intervention comes with a

need for *learning* – which always takes time and practice. And since anything new has to work with what's already there, delays and difficulties are inevitable as you fit things together. So persistence and focus are crucial, whereas impatience and a short-run orientation are potentially crippling.

They "lead to fads," cautions MIT professor emeritus Edgar Schein, "a preoccupation with instant solutions, a blind faith that if we put in enough effort and money anything is possible, and an unwillingness and inability to see the long-range consequences of some of the quick fixes which we try."[3]

No need for predictable surprises

Over the past century, countless people have claimed to understand what makes companies tick and what makes some more competitive than others. They've produced, packaged, and peddled a truly astonishing amount of advice. But the outcome of their efforts is invariably another minor tweak to *existing* knowledge rather than the invention of something new.

It is true that significant insights and ideas have been produced in areas such as finance, accounting, marketing, operations, and decision-making. But in the two areas whose impact on business performance overshadows all others – strategy and people management – we've seen little progress. Our understanding of how to compete and win evolves at a glacial pace. The breakthroughs would fill a thimble.

Most of what's touted as "thought leadership" is, in fact, "thought *followership*." It hitches a ride on what we already know, perhaps from a slightly different angle, or dressed up with a new name or information from a new study, but adds little to our understanding of how to manage for advantage. With few exceptions, "new" ideas are at best marginal when it comes to utility. The language describing them might change, but the foundational concepts hold firm.

Bluntly put: in one of humankind's most crucial areas of knowledge and practice, we're going nowhere slowly.

The good news is that most of what spews forth never reaches managers. The bad news is that much of what does reach them is confusing rather than enlightening; distracting at best, useless at worst. All too often, this results in unnecessary costs and work rather than better business results.

This could be a crisis, but it doesn't have to be.

As Max Bazerman and Michael Watkins point out in their book *Predictable Surprises*, "a predictable surprise arises when leaders unquestionably had all the data and insight they needed to recognize the potential for, even the inevitability of, a crisis, but failed to respond with effective preventative action."[4]

We know what we need to know about management. It is clear what practices we need, and we have them already.

There is no need to create nasty surprises for ourselves by persisting in a hunt for different truths.

The right question

Starting in the early 1980s, I became interested in understanding:

- Why do some companies, facing similar challenges to others, stand out from the crowd and consistently get superior results?
- Why, with so much information and advice about management so easily, widely, and quickly available, is corporate performance so different from company to company, and so erratic within them?

- Why is *failure* – of products, projects, and firms themselves – so common?
- Why do popular management ideas seem to work in some organizations, but not others?

These questions have challenged many people. You don't have to look far to find opinions on all of them. But you do need to carefully weigh those up, and not be too quick to assume any answer to be the right one or the final word on the matter. Strong views are sure to prompt further research, bringing new information and interpretations. What appears to hold true at one moment, and to make absolute sense, will inevitably be disputed and possibly refuted.

As the business context changes, so do fashions in business thinking. At any time, certain issues and ideas hold the high ground and crowd out others; then those are displaced and different ones hold sway. Overarching themes such as globalization, outsourcing and offshoring (and now, *re*shoring* and *next*-shoring†), sustainability, empowerment, diversity, emerging markets, or inclusive growth take hold and shift strategic conversations in new directions. Ideas about how to manage burst onto the scene, stir a flurry of activity, then give way to others. What's "trending" today is ho-hum or forgotten tomorrow.

One way to deal with my questions was to stay with them, perhaps even add more, and keep probing. Another was to get more specific and ask fewer questions. The first option would be

* Bringing operations back to a home country.

† A McKinsey term invented to highlight the need to decide whether to manufacture close to sources of innovation or to customers.

interesting but unlikely to produce what I wanted any time soon, so I quickly abandoned it. The second would cut to the chase.

So I asked, "What's the *intent* of my initial questions? What exactly am I trying to find out and explain?" This prompted me to narrow my search and explore three new questions:

1. What do winning companies do that also-rans don't?
2. Does success depend on particular management practices, and are they necessary in all companies?
3. Do we know what we need to know about them?

Concentrating my efforts refuelled my belief that we were over-complicating things, repeating ourselves, and searching for answers we didn't need. That in our desperation to pump up business performance, we were overreaching – and *impeding* performance.

In most organizations, too many concepts, tools, and initiatives compete for attention. Managers themselves create too much work. And much of it doesn't meld into a coherent process.

So I began to wonder if there were *imperatives* – things firms *must* do, not what they say they do or would like to do. Ideas that have stood the test of time and matter everywhere. Practices that would focus management attention where it is most needed and would have the most impact.

This brought me to just one question:

Are there *must-do* practices that make companies competitive, and if so, what are they?

The truth is well hidden

It would be impossible to consider every scrap of knowledge about a subject as broad as management, or every factor influencing business outcomes. There are many aspects to managing, and they're bound up with each other and with a host of exogenous factors over which executives have little or no control.

Part art, part craft, part science, management involves analysis and logic, imagination, instinct, attitude, skill, luck – and more. All of which makes it hard to put your finger on the exact causes of specific business results.

Inevitably, one element such as culture or strategy gets highlighted, while others such as resource endowments, patents, past commitments, timing, or luck are overlooked or downplayed. Or a leader's humility, decisiveness, or foresight is singled out as her great strength – and the reason for her success – when the truth lies elsewhere. Or executives claim that one or other theory or tool worked for them, when in reality it played only a minor role in their success, or none at all. So it's common for firms held up as exemplars one year to hit the skids the next (think Enron, ABB, Nokia, Bear Stearns, Kodak, Dell, Tesco, or Monitor Consulting – the list is endless). Even analysts whose job it is to study particular firms and tell investors about their prospects are often hopelessly wrong.

The influence and longevity of management ideas differ greatly. Some have a short shelf life: they take off fast, but never gain traction and quickly vanish. Some come and go, then reappear. Very few top the charts and stay there. You'd think those that have made it so far would be worth paying attention to.

And you have to wonder why they're not.

There are more fads and flaky ideas in management than reliable guidance, so finding the good stuff is a challenge. A wealth of studies claim to tell us what works, but their rigour and value vary. There are gems among them, certainly, but there's also dross.

A lot of what passes for "management research" is deeply flawed, and even apparently thorough efforts to get to the truth can yield dodgy results.

Many success recipes are rustled up by people who skim over the surface of organizations and scoop up stories, analogies, or other "evidence" to make a point. The greatest strength of these authors is their ability to coin aphorisms that grab attention and stick in your mind, to spin a gripping yarn, or to weave seductive arguments from the flimsiest of raw material.

But the fact that some idea is put on a pedestal or appears to be widely used doesn't mean it leads to whatever results are attributed to it. Popularity surveys are unlikely to yield the answers managers crave, as hype often outweighs common sense.

The fact that a business book becomes a bestseller is no assurance of new thinking, and may say nothing about the practical worth of the contents. You can't assume that reprint orders for journal articles – or even citations – are testimony to originality or merit. Or that success on the speaking circuit is evidence of a useful message. For once any halfway decent idea becomes public and starts creating a buzz, its author will inevitably be joined by others, many with their own take on it. But "the wisdom of crowds" might reflect no more than opportunism or a herd mentality at work.

When something is repeated often enough or loudly enough, there's a chance it'll come to be seen as reality. This happens a lot in the management advice industry. What seems to get results for one business is copied by others, and gets some press. Someone picks up on what's happening, and claims to know the reason. This gets more attention, and triggers more "studies" – and the next thing you know, a "theory" is born.

Then the noise rises. Managers clamour for information about this new silver bullet. As the numbers using it grow, it gains "best practice" status. If anyone is bothered by its dubious pedigree, they either say nothing or voice (often in a whisper) their concern in some academic journal where it's unnoticed and soon forgotten.

So what *are* harried executives to believe?

Are the prescriptions they need the eight from *In Search of Excellence*?[5] The nine from *Built to Last*?[6] The three from *The Discipline of Market Leaders*?[7] The seven from *Good to Great*,[8] or the six from *Great by Choice*[9] (both books authored by Jim Collins)? Or what about the five from *Staying Power*?[10] Or perhaps the "four + two" from *What Really Works*?[11] The seven from *Vanguard Management*?[12] The nine from *The Agenda*?[13] "The Four Principles of Enduring Success," advocated by Christian Stadler in a *Harvard Business Review* article?[14*] Or the "Three Rules for Making a Company Truly Great," from another *HBR* article, by Michael E. Raynor and Mumtaz Ahmed?[15]

All these formulas are the outcome of hard labour by really clever people. But who's right? The criteria for "success" and the methodology for understanding it differ from one of these studies to the next. There is sound advice in all of them. But although there are some overlaps, there are sharp differences too.

So how might we decide which list to go with?

Can we choose, or do we need them all?

Do *all* companies need to go the same route?

Would it make sense to cherry-pick ideas we fancy, and cobble them together into a new list?

---

* He added a fifth rule in a follow-up book (*Enduring Success*, Stanford: Stanford University Press, 2011), but I'm only including four here.

Or – here's a worry! – maybe *none* of these is what we need. After all, there's a plethora of advice hidden in the dark corners of management literature. Maybe there are other ideas we haven't heard of, that haven't been sexily packaged, or that haven't been given the recognition they deserve.

Opinions are everywhere. But which to consider?

I have no doubt that many people will swear they were helped by these books and articles. Many more will read them in future and join their fan clubs.

But note this:

Between them, those publications list a total of 70 prescripts that apparently give winning firms their edge (see Appendix). Their authors make a persuasive case for each of them, and it's easy to see why they've proved attractive to a great many managers. However, only a handful of them qualify for the "must-do" label. The rest are optional extras you may be tempted to adopt and that might boost your business – or not. Some might be usefully *added* to more fundamental practices, but are no substitute for them. None will do you much good if you don't have the basics in place first, and work at them relentlessly.

And it's those basics I'll tell you about here.

My screening process

As you can imagine, it would be possible with little effort to mention countless concepts and cite hundreds of renowned experts, and even more examples and stories of what apparently worked where, when, and how, and what didn't. But since strategy and people, more than anything else, stood out as the most important determinants of business results, they were my focus.

As I progressed, I filtered what I learned through an imaginary "sieve" (Figure 1.2) to identify insights or ideas that:

1. Were *original* – not repeated, rehashed, or rebranded.
2. Had *endured* over multiple years.
3. Had been *rigorously studied and validated.*
4. *Underpinned the latest thinking* about management.
5. Were *critical* to the performance of a company.
6. Were *generic* in that they applied across countries, companies, and industries.
7. Were *required in all circumstances.*
8. Were likely to *remain* critical in the future.

Figure 1.2

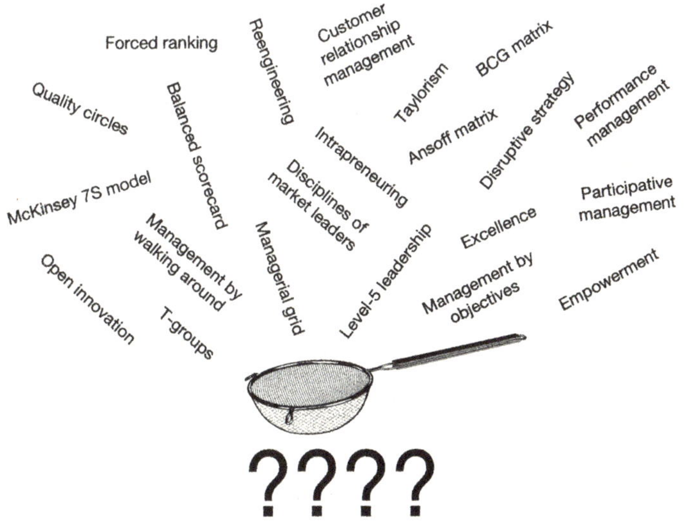

What fell through as I trawled the history of management ideas were eight practices – the essence of 100 years of management thought:

#1. **Growth leadership** – Effective leadership that's committed to growth, and to achieving it by growing people.
#2. **Fast learning and adaptation** – The ability to sense and make sense of change, and to act on it and learn from it faster than competitors.
#3. **Focus, value, costs** – Clarity about where and how to compete, and a relentless effort to drive value up and costs down for the "right" customer.
#4. **Business model innovation** – Continual reinvention of the way value is created, delivered, captured, and shared.
#5. **Resource and capability acquisition, development, and leverage** – Accessing, attracting, acquiring, and building the strengths needed to compete, and using them to maximum effect.
#6. **Stakeholder alignment and support** – Persuading individuals and organizations with any interest in a firm to "vote" for it rather than against it.
#7. **Smart sequencing and pacing** – Doing the right things in the right order and at the right time.
#8. **Disciplined execution** – Employing a deliberate and systematic way to turn intentions into action and results (Figure 1.3).

These practices appeared time and again, in different guises or explained in different ways. There was no escaping them. And if one expert or observer after another was saying much the same thing – sometimes decades apart, and maybe couched in different terms and presented from a fresh angle, in a different context, or with fresh evidence and reasoning – then surely that meant something.

And indeed it does.

Figure 1.3

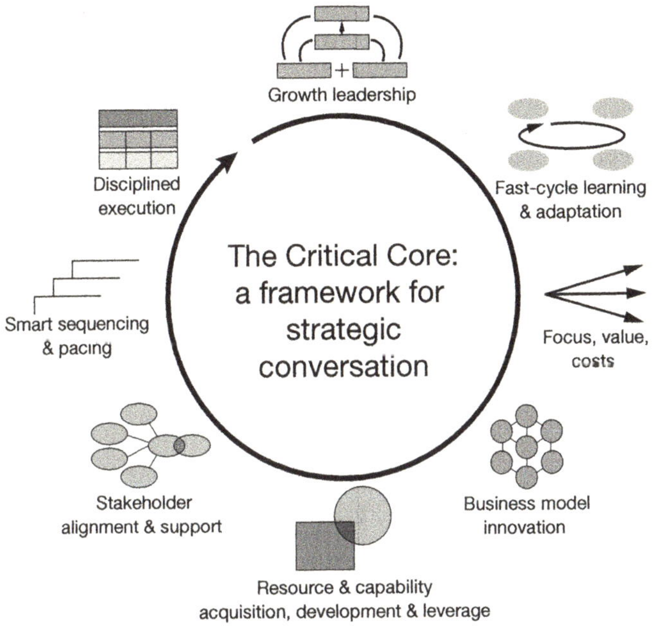

Together, the practices add up to *a way of working* that involves all your people. As *an interdependent system*, they help you frame your strategic conversation and ensure that you give your full attention to the activities that really will produce superior results. They also provide a useful means by which to unpack and understand your competitors' strategies. (And they can be used by investors, analysts, and journalists to make sense of a firm's current situation and its prospects.)

At first glance, you might see this as an obvious and underwhelming list. You might, as one professor did, dismiss these practices as mere "tickets to the game," so rudimentary as to not be worth a second glance. But that would be a huge mistake. They not only get you into the game, but also keep you there, and enable you to win. And hardly a day goes by without news of businesses that have lost their way or failed because:

- Their leaders lack the will or skill to grow, and the growth of their people is not their priority (Practice #1).
- The world around them changes faster than they do (Practice #2).
- They're unfocused, don't make a difference that matters to customers, don't keep offering them new value, and don't keep driving their costs down (Practice #3).
- Their business models are ineffective, and become obsolete (Practice #4).
- They don't acquire or develop the resources and capabilities they need, and don't leverage them to get the most bang for their bucks (Practice #5).
- Their stakeholders are at odds with them (Practice #6).
- They act without a sense of what to do and when to do it (Practice #7).
- They're unable to implement their plans (Practice #8).

On the other hand, it would be a stretch to argue that any firm failed as a direct result of *not* using some high-profile tool such as a BCG matrix or five-forces analysis, *kaizen*, CRM, or design thinking. Helpful though any of these may be, not using them might not matter. They're means to an end, not an end in themselves. And there are many other ways to skin a cat.

Success, *insofar as managers can determine it*, depends 100 per cent on the eight critical practices. The same cannot be said of almost any other management idea.

The way the practices were *applied* 100 years ago – or even a month or a week ago – was unquestionably and often radically different than the way it's done today. But you can't get away from the fact that the practices, both singly and in combination, are now more critical than ever. In fact, they're *obligatory.*

But aren't there many besides these eight that you need to consider?

You're probably itching to add others. But when you subject them to the various tests I used, it'll be apparent that they don't warrant being termed "critical." They may help you *implement* these practices, but if that's not your express intention, you don't need them. Blurring the distinction between *must-do* and *nice-to-do* leads you straight into the very trap you should avoid: of jamming too many tools into your management toolkit, and too much onto your action list.

This is not to say that mastering the practices will on its own guarantee your success. Of course it won't. Strategy isn't a simple paint-by-numbers process. It's dynamic and full of surprises, as it occurs within a complex environment and is subject to countless variables. Whatever ideas you use are only as good as the human skills with which you apply them.

But what is clear is that what we need to know about management is a lot less complicated than it's made out to be.

When Peter Drucker got his first consulting assignment, a massive study of General Motors, in 1943, he "knew nothing about management. I gave myself a quickie course," he recalled, "finding to my surprise that I could read all of the significant books about management in two days. There were just seven books on general management ... and most of them repeated each other."[16]

Now, 70-plus years later, we have more information about the topic than Drucker would ever have imagined. But "significant"? Less than you might think. Repetition? Volumes of it.

While I was thinking about all this and bouncing my thoughts off various people, three things happened that convinced me I was on the right track.

First came a number of articles, books, seminars, and conferences about "management innovation," which generated a great deal of excitement but fell short on actual progress.

Then came the global financial crisis, which turned into a deep and protracted economic slump, taking companies by surprise and forcing them to rethink their management beliefs and scramble for salvation in both emergency surgery and new ideas.

And, third, it became evident that the business models which had worked so well for many firms were suddenly under threat from challengers who were upending the status quo in one industry after another.

All this brought me to the conclusion on which this book is based:

> *What firms need today is not new ways to manage so much as to apply what's already known and proved to work. There is a core set of eight management practices that have been around for decades, and have been shown to positively affect business results. They're "generic," in the sense that they apply to all companies worldwide, and they're critical, not optional. These practices encompass virtually everything a firm does to compete. Together they comprise a "strategy system" in which various tools and techniques can be used to achieve specific aims, and provide a frame for effective strategic conversation.*

Of course, a statement like this won't go unchallenged. It will irk anyone involved in the study of management, and disappoint managers itching for breakthroughs.

But consider why each practice is necessary ... and what the alternative might be (Figure 1.4).

Figure 1.4

THE CRITICAL STRATEGY PRACTICES	WHAT THEY MEAN	THE ALTERNATIVE
#1. Growth leadership	Leadership that is committed to growth, and to achieving it by growing people	Leaders not driven by growth, or not committed to delivering it through the growth of their people
#2. Fast learning & adaptation	Sense, understand, and act on change – and *learn* from the process – faster than your competitors	Fail to see or understand changes in your world, and respond to them in your own good time
#3. Focus, value, costs	Focus on the "right" customer, and relentlessly drive value up and costs down	Chase everyone ("spray and pray") with offerings they don't value, while driving that value down and your costs up
#4. Business model innovation	Constantly redesign the way value is created, delivered, and captured	Stick with business as usual – more of the same even when it no longer works
#5. Resource & capability acquisition, development & leverage	Acquire, access, and grow the resources and capabilities you need to compete, and get the most from them	Go into battle with forces that are ill-equipped and lack the skills to win, and fail to use all your firepower
#6. Stakeholder alignment & support	Create win-win relationships to get all stakeholders on your side	Leave stakeholders to pursue their own agendas ... maybe to work against you
#7. Smart sequencing & pacing	Do the right things in the right order, and at the right time	Do everything all at once, as fast as you can or as slowly as you like
#8. Disciplined execution	Employ a systematic approach to getting the right things done	Set vague goals, assign no clear responsibilities, apply no pressure for results, shift priorities, and tolerate non-delivery

Testing. Testing. Testing

How sure can you be that all this is true? *Because the best evidence we have about management says so.*

Whether it's from executives, employees, academics, consultants, journalists, books, peer-reviewed journals, or wherever, nothing contradicts it.

The eight practices that meet my search criteria are the core of all management thinking and recur constantly in management literature. But that alone couldn't be a reason to highlight them.

So I turned to five well-known tests of management ideas. And I added two more because the practical nature of the topic means that knowledge for the sake of knowledge cannot be enough. Visible, meaningful results must follow (Figure 1.5).

Figure 1.5

TESTS OF MANAGEMENT THEORY

The accepted criteria

1. **It should have a sound base.** The sample size, methodology, and evidence should provide confidence in it.
2. **It should have predictive power.** ("If you do A you'll get B.")
3. **It should have explanatory power.** ("This is why A causes B.")
4. **It should "travel."** It should lead to similar outcomes across different organizations, in different industries and countries.
5. **The circumstances in which it works or doesn't work, and the reasons, should be clear.** ("It works when A, B, or C are happening, but not D, E, or F – and this is why.")

My additional criteria

6. **It should be practical.** Managers need to be able to use it.
7. **It should significantly advance the practice of management.**

Every one of the eight practices passes every test.

Still not satisfied? Well, turn back to page 29 and apply my initial eight-point test. Or consider the alternatives to these practices (Figure 1.4).

Again, every one of the eight critical strategy practices passes on all counts.

Now, combine those practices into one joined-up approach to managing your business and apply those tests to it.

And again, a 100 per cent pass!

This book isn't based on interesting commonalities among a handful of companies. Nor have I picked a tool or technique that seemed to work here or there, and suggested it could work for everyone. But what I have got to is a set of practices that have been shown, again and again over many decades, by countless experts, to apply across companies, industries, and countries. A set of practices that, separately and together, meet every accepted test of a management theory – plus two of my own.

These practices are not just necessary, but *critical* to every organization. I've found no example of any firm – in books, articles, annual reports, case studies, business school classes, or wherever – that did well while flouting them. And of the hundreds of companies I've consulted to, I can't think of one that might have done better by doing something else.

There is no time, place, or circumstance in which the practices don't matter or won't assist management performance – except when managers fail to apply them well.

No manager can afford to pass up the potentially positive impact of these practices.

No manager can rationally say, "The practices don't apply to me," or "They won't work in my industry," or "I have better things to do."

Nor can they afford to wait for some guru to come up with smarter answers. For much as the possibility of a great leap forward might excite executives under pressure to improve results, the likelihood of one appearing is slim to zero.

Everything you know about strategy and management – every concept, tool, technique, model, framework, or whatever – is peripheral to the eight critical strategy practices. If you don't work at these, nothing else matters. If you do work at them, all those other things become more useful and more effective.

The impact on learning and development

The development of managerial skills is a major challenge to any firm. Yet often it's left to chance. And even where it appears to be deliberate, it's mostly an unstructured, ad hoc, and sporadic process which leaves people with a scattering of tools, no linkage between them, and no clear understanding of how to use them. From a smorgasbord of courses, seminars, and workshops, exposure to experts, reading, workplace socializing, and experience, they pick up ideas and develop their own beliefs about how to manage. Little of what they learn is transferred into the workplace. And there's scant effort to calculate the return on investment, even if it were possible.

Given what's at stake, this makes no sense. If, instead, companies used the critical strategy practices as a framework for management development, they would be better off in three ways:

1. Their approach to development would be consistent and coherent, and their people would learn what really matters. With everyone exposed to the same set of ideas, they'd have a common language and communication would be improved.
2. By promoting one management approach rather than letting everyone go their own way, they'd be able to give their full attention to deepening the expertise of individuals and of their organization as a whole in the critical practices.
3. They would facilitate faster, more effective learning. "In order for someone to capture complex, experience-based knowledge,"

say Dorothy Leonard and Walter Swap in their book *Deep Smarts*, "the person's brain has to contain receptors – neural structures that are the physical representations of frameworks, domain knowledge, or prior experiences – to which the current inputs can be connected."[17] Similarly, Lev Semyonovich Vygotsky, a 20th-century developmental psychologist, wrote of the importance of "scaffolding," or systematic support, in helping children learn. Initially, he said, it would come from an outsider, but later should be a product of internal conversations.[18]

The eight critical practices provide the "receptors" or "scaffolding" people need to receive, stack, store, and retrieve information and experience. Give them these as a starting point, and they have something to build on.

In a 1959 *Harvard Business Review* article, "Thinking Ahead: Potentials of Management Science," Drucker wrote:

> Managing will always remain somewhat of an "art"; the talent, experience, vision, courage, and character of the managers will always be major factors in their performance and that of their enterprise. But this is true of medicine and doctors, too. And, as with medicine, management and managers – especially the most highly endowed and most highly accomplished managers – will become the more effective as their foundation of organized systematic knowledge and organized systematic search grows stronger, and as their roots in a real discipline of management and entrepreneurship grow deeper. That such a discipline is possible, the work already done in management science proves.
>
> But no one, I am also convinced, can survey the work to date without being worried at the same time. The potential is there – but it is in danger of being frittered away. Instead of a

> management science which supplies knowledge, concepts, and discipline to manager and entrepreneur, we may be developing a "management gadget bag" of techniques for the efficiency expert.[19]

More than 50 years later, when terms like speed, agility, resilience, responsiveness, and adaptability trip so freely from the tongues of managers, that "management gadget bag" has become a dead weight on their performance. Yet life doesn't need to be so hard.

We have the foundation of knowledge that we need.

What's left is to *apply* it.

First steps to new results

Albert Einstein famously said, "It is insanity to keep doing the same thing and expect different results." So if you want new sales and profits, you need to start by asking, "What must we do differently to get those results?"

My answer:

Embed and master the critical strategy practices into your organization by using them to frame your strategic conversation.

This probably means you need to change many things.

During the years I've worked to learn about management, clarify what we know about strategy, simplify how we make and implement it, and help my clients craft and conduct effective strategic conversations, I've become increasingly sure that if leaders want to make a difference, they should:

- **Dump a lot of what they *think* they know about managing and get to work with what we really *do* know.**

- **Sweep aside most of their current theories, fads, themes, and tools, "clear the decks," and make a fresh start.** Clutter is distracting and slows things down.
- **Fight complexity for all they're worth.** Simplicity is their friend and they need to embrace it, worship it, and live it.
- **Accept that great results come slowly and settle in for the long haul.** Business success is hardly ever an overnight matter. For most firms, it comes over time, through relentless practice, experimentation, learning, improvement, adaptation, and resource and capacity building.

We'll return later to some detail about the eight critical practices. Meanwhile, test your strategic fitness using the following score sheet (Figure 1.6), and keep checking your performance over coming months.

Figure 1.6

TEST YOUR STRATEGIC FITNESS						
PRACTICE	RATING					SCORE
	1	2	3	4	5	
#1. Growth leadership						
#2. Fast learning & adaptation						
#3. Focus, value, costs						
#4. Business model innovation						
#5. Resource & capability acquisition, development & leverage						
#6. Stakeholder alignment & support						
#7. Smart sequencing & pacing						
#8. Disciplined execution						
TOTAL						/40
Rate your company on each practice, using the 1–5 scale, where 1 = poor and 5 = excellent. Total the scores: maximum 40 points.						

2

ESSENTIAL PRINCIPLES

Well, you've been warned. With the keen help of the management advice industry, you run the risk of flummoxing yourself, complicating your management approach, and burdening your organization with theories and tools that won't help you get the results you want. There's a very real possibility that your ideas about strategy and the way you make strategy already hurt rather than help your performance.

There are many ways to think about strategy. Most centre on how to make smart decisions while sidestepping the fact that it's human beings – with all their foibles and fallibilities – who make and execute those decisions. A plethora of tools assist with the analysis of markets, customers, competitors, and value chains. Others provide systematic ways to tackle issues that range from organizational design and innovation to productivity and quality. Their technical flavour is reassuring in a messy world, and they promise a safe and sure path to success.

But don't be duped. Aside from other weaknesses, their very purpose is to simplify things.* And what they omit can be far more important than what they include.

Simplicity is imperative in organizational matters. But it's only a hop and a skip from there to being dangerously *simplistic* – to relying on naive and one-dimensional thinking that disregards the realities of working in a dynamic system with multiple actors, and with entangled feedback loops that multiply as you work. So even as you strip away complexity, you need to accept it and embrace it. Only when analysis meets synthesis is it possible to come out on top in a VUCA environment.

---

* My own models, which feature in this book, do the same. Hence my constant emphasis of contextual sensitivity in thinking about strategy, and of the human factors that take decisions in one direction or another.

Crafting a strategy is nowhere near as straightforward as following a recipe to make a chicken pie. (And even with the same recipe, two cooks won't necessarily get the same results.) Successfully *executing* strategy involves insights, emotions, power, politics, attitudes, aspirations, relationships, judgment, skill, and many other human factors. It always requires learning and adaptation. Context always plays an overriding role.

Crafting and conducting a strategic conversation is not a straight-line, box-ticking exercise that can be wrapped up in a prescribed time, or that comes to a definite ending. It's a convoluted, iterative process that happens in boardrooms and retreats, at office coffee machines and in the gym. It involves one-word text messages and one-line emails, passage chats and drawn-out meetings, and teleconferences and PowerPoint presentations. It moves along in fits and starts, doubles back, and twists and turns in unexpected directions. Decisions born from hours of agonizing in a workshop may be overturned before you get back to the office. Months of data gathering and analysis may be no match for gut feel or lucky breaks. A single customer visit can have more impact on your future direction than a consultant's costly report. An accidental insight or serendipitous encounter can change the course of history. Grand plans that emerge from the C-suite may fizzle in light of remarks by someone in an executive's family.

However, no company can do well for long by bumbling along and dabbling in this and that, and just waiting to see what happens. There has to be some clarity about its purpose and intentions, and certainty and coherence in what it does. This requires hard choices, which have to be made deliberately rather than by default.

But there also has to be an openness to new information and ideas, and a willingness to take them on board and change direction in a heartbeat.

Striking this balance is never easy. Your best hope lies in a management approach that's based on the critical core, and that combines patience with decisiveness.

But before we go there, let's consider some essential principles that will help you. I've written about many of them for a long time. As with the eight critical strategy practices, they apply to every company, everywhere.

PRINCIPLE #1: Every decision must pass the Ten-Buck Test

All strategy involves the commitment of resources for a future you can't see.

Like you and me, companies have limited resources and many possibilities for using them. So managers have to make difficult choices and trade-offs, and, whenever possible, apply resources to opportunities, not problems. They have to say yes to some things, but no to even more.

Doing everything is not an option. Trying to do too much is a key cause of failure.

When you lose focus and lapse into "spray and pray" mode, you court trouble. Instead of excelling in one important thing, you inevitably become mediocre or hopeless at many.[1]

Think about this as making bets for tomorrow, "ten bucks" at a time. And make it a habit to subject every business decision – about how you spend your time; and about products, markets, people, technologies, structures, systems, processes, projects, contracts, or whatever – to what I call the Ten-Buck Test. Just ask, "Is this the best way to use our ten bucks?" If it's not, you probably shouldn't do it.

Every bet is a risk. But every bet is also a *learning opportunity*, for whether they turn out well or badly, they teach you something. Making them is the only way to move your firm forward, and to build the physical and mental muscle you need to compete. The faster you do this the better, especially when you and your competitors are all doing more or less the same things.

This brings us to two concepts that can either make or break a business.

Strategic bets come with different levels of risk and reward. What they all share is that once made, they become "sunk costs." Some are easily reversible, and with no serious consequences. Others offer no escape.

Ideally, as they add up, they make your firm stronger and give you a *rational* reason to keep going – and to commit even more to the same course. But if things go awry, *emotion* may stifle common sense and keep you moving in the wrong direction. "We've come this far and invested so much, we can't quit now," you tell yourself. "Another few steps, and the big payoff will come."

But the payoff you seek may never come.

On the contrary, the further you continue down the same disappointing path, the more vulnerable you can make your firm. Your bets lead to what economists call "path dependence," with successive commitments locking you ever more tightly into a particular course of action – and thus making it more difficult to *change* direction.[2] The very doggedness that's so vital to success can ensure your downfall.

Deep and valuable knowledge about an industry, markets, and customers can't be plucked off a shelf. Figuring out how to compete, and designing and fine-tuning the business model you need, doesn't happen overnight. It takes time and hard work to develop resources, capabilities, infrastructure, and relationships, and when these are combined they can give you a competitive advantage that can't be easily or quickly copied.

So while sunk costs and path dependence may lead to outcomes you don't want, you can't live without them. But best you think about them early, and try to anticipate their effects and mitigate whatever risks may come with them.

Strategy provides a context for your bets and helps you weigh them up before you make them. But your strategy has to be clear and specific to do this. If, like many of the executives I meet, you fail to show 100 per cent commitment to a purpose, or keep changing your mind about where you want to take your firm and how you'll get there, you'll squander energy and effort. Necessary as "thinking out of the box" may be, it becomes the enemy of results when it gets more airtime than "Focus! Focus! Focus!"

PRINCIPLE #2:
It's all about framing

Peter Drucker effectively defined strategy when he counselled executives to constantly ask themselves, "What is our business, and what should it be?" And when he urged them to get to the answers by stepping outside of their business and asking three further questions: "Who is our customer? What is value to them? How can we deliver it?"

Strategy is as much about choosing a favourable market position as it is about choosing and executing the activities that will deliver the promise of that position. So it all comes down to sense-making – *the creation and communication of a point of view about where and how a firm will compete.*[3]

The common factor in all this is people.

They create and implement strategy. Strategy guides them.

As Chester Barnard observed in his 1938 book *The Functions of the Executive*, companies are social organizations, and "the first executive function is to develop and maintain a system of communication."[4]

Such a system requires common language, clear messages, and an effective process. Providing these is the work of leaders – of strategists. Their effectiveness depends on how they frame and reframe what their organization is about: its *situation*, the central *challenge* it must deal with, its *theory of success*, and the *activities* and *actions* in which it must excel.[5]

By crafting and conducting their strategic conversation around these four issues, *with constant reference to the eight critical practices,* they determine what gets talked about, and thus what gets attention and what gets done (Figure 2.1).

Figure 2.1

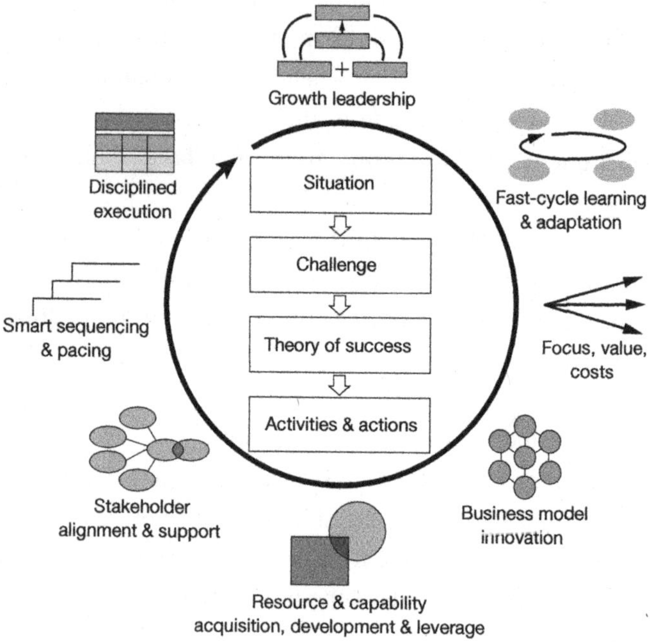

1. Your situation. In crafting your strategy, nothing is more important than understanding the current state of your organization and its environment, having a sense of how both might change, and knowing what stands between you and success.

To sensibly decide where you want to take your company, and how best to do it – and to manage the risks you'll surely encounter – you need to know as much as possible about conditions in and around your organization, and what may lie ahead.

This knowledge won't guarantee success. But it does give you a sound basis on which to define your strategic challenge, set realistic goals, decide which activities you must excel in, and ascertain your priorities. Uncertainty, on the other hand, will lead to a lack of focus and so to unnecessary costs, waste, and inefficiencies. And the less you know, the more likely it is that things will go wrong.

The way you frame your firm's situation does more than inform decisions. It also sets a *tone* within your organization, so it affects the attitude of people around you.

You could, for example, portray the overall outlook as being either encouraging or grim. Or you could speak of the economy, competition, new regulation, a technology trend, or a shift in buyer behaviour as presenting either problems or opportunities. What you choose to focus on, the facts you use, and how you pitch your story all add up to a particular impression.

Whether you're upbeat or downbeat will influence how people feel, which in turn will affect their behaviour; so you have to be mindful of how you come across. Initial impressions are sticky, and you may not be able to easily erase them. Actions do speak louder than words, and framing is about far more than just making a speech. Everything you do and the way you do everything sends signals, and the people around you watch like hawks to decode what you really mean.

A host of factors affect the way you see your situation. First, there's the mass of *facts, impressions, opinions, and insights* you glean from social interactions, news, reading, seminars, presentations, social media, debates with colleagues, customer visits, and innumerable other sources. This is your raw material, and you need lots of it. Then there are your *cognitive capabilities* – your mental processing power. And finally, there are *filters* such as your natural optimism or pessimism, and your mental models, values, prejudices, preferences, and experience.

These shape not only your perceptions of your current reality, but also your assumptions about the future – and thus how you define your strategic challenge. So this is where you can begin to distinguish yourself from your competitors.

Even though you and they may both have access to the same information, it's *what you do with it* that makes the difference. Cognitive capability and filters cause the same raw material to mean different things to different people. So faced with the same objective circumstances, you and your rivals are likely to arrive at different views of "the truth." The version you choose defines your strategy and powerfully influences the actions that follow.

This brings us to a paradox that every leader must embrace:

Napoleon is reputed to have said, "A leader is a dealer in hope" – his point being that you need to promise better times ahead, or no one will follow you. But former General Electric chairman Jack Welch, in typically blunt fashion, admonished leaders to "look the future in the eye, and see the reality that is, not the one you want to see."

Both statements are valid, and you have to keep them both in mind when you discuss your strategy. Crafting and conducting a strategic conversation demands hard facts and a willingness to confront them. But it's your *attitude*, the way you project your message – and above all, your *actions* – that determine how those facts are perceived, and hence how they influence behaviour.

Some firms are able to break all records in terrible conditions, while others go out of business. The difference might lie in strategy, or in resources and capabilities, but *the way leaders choose to frame their situation invariably plays a part.* It's the decider more often than you think.

This is not to say you should try to put a gloss on all bad news, or pretend all's well when everyone can see it's not. Honesty and straight talk can't be optional extras in strategic conversation. Without them, it's impossible to do the right things. You need them for effective decisions, and even more for effective execution of those decisions. If you refuse to confront reality, or massage facts to concoct a "reality" you like, you'll create risks and destroy trust. And you'll soon be found out.

A clear understanding of your situation might be exactly what you need to light a fire under your team and spur them to action. But avoid dwelling on the difficulties you face, and rather focus on what you and your team can *do* about them. Talk less about the past than the future. Use the way things *are* as a means to get to *what they could be.*

In an old joke that Ronald Reagan used to tell, a farmer finds his little boy digging through a pile of manure in the barn on Christmas Day. "What are you doing?" he asks. And the kid answers, "If there's manure around here, there's got to be a pony!"

Strategy is about finding that pony.

2. Your challenge. The first question in strategy seems an obvious one: *Why exactly do you need a strategy?* If you fail to address this up front, and don't develop a clear and concise view of the specific challenge you must deal with, any subsequent conversation will lack focus. You won't be able to remember or communicate the purpose of your strategy, and you and your team will run around aimlessly.

Maybe there's a spectacular *opportunity* ahead. Maybe there are signs the economy is about to improve, and a surge in sales is likely. Maybe you're poised to enter a foreign market, exploit a new technology or distribution channel, strike up a new partnership, or merge with another firm. All of these call for particular actions.

On the other hand, what if you're swamped by *problems*? Or even just *one* problem? What if a competitor has suddenly become more aggressive, and is adding factory capacity, opening new sales outlets, cutting prices, and targeting your best customers? Or your business model is no longer "fit for purpose"? Or customers are deserting you, your sales are vaporizing, and your firm's survival is at stake?

Again, in every case, you need to be clear about the specific challenge you face, so you can craft your strategy and focus your resources accordingly.

You can't do everything, so you need to narrow down the possibilities.

3. Your theory of success. Strategy is an *intention*, not a fact. Until you act it out, you have no idea whether or how well it'll work. But if you don't start with an opinion about what you're trying to achieve, and which activities and actions will get you there, you'll have no basis for planning your way forward or designing your business model. You won't know what to focus on.

Your theory of success defines what you mean by success, and what's needed to achieve it.[6] You might think you have one, but even if you do, chances are it's *implicit* rather than *explicit*, and fuzzy rather than precise – which isn't helpful. Only if you are totally aware of your recipe and its logic, can easily spell it out to people who need to know it, and refer to it often, will it be a useful tool.

This means, as always, that simplicity and clarity are paramount. So don't get bogged down in infinite detail. Forget about writing a multi-page essay. Get to the point: "This is the result we want. So this is what we must do, and why, and how."

You might not be able to pare down your thoughts to "one moving part" (to borrow from Drucker), but the closer you can get to that, the better.

4. Your key activities and actions. The analysis and thought you put into your strategy has one ultimate goal: to ascertain the activities on which you should focus your ten bucks, and the actions that will turn them into strengths and bring the results you want. This is where the rubber meets the road, and where winners emerge. Get this right, and you're off to a good start – instead of continuing to worry about *what* to do, you can forge ahead with *doing*. But get it wrong, and once again focus will go out of the window.

The activities you elect to perform must each have a specific purpose. They must also enhance each other, and they must function as a whole. So they must be chosen, designed, and configured individually, but with the *complete system* in mind. The same applies to your actions. Only through such symbiosis will you get the most bang for your ten bucks.

If your point of view about where and how to compete is to be of any worth, it has to be based on facts, logic, and common sense. You have to be able to explain it fast. And as far as possible, your audience needs to understand it as you do, and be as convinced by it as you are.

There are many ways to develop and package strategy, but few match the simple, sound, and practical approach outlined here. Instead of brevity, they bring verbosity. Instead of simplicity, they bring complexity. Instead of clarity, they bring confusion. Instead of cutting to the chase and telling people, "We're going to take that hill, for this reason, by doing A, B, and C," they leave them wondering, "Where are we going? Does it make sense? Can we do it?"

And, most concerning, "So what am *I* supposed to do?"

I'm firmly convinced, by overwhelming evidence from myriad sources – and especially from my own interactions with thousands of managers and many more people who report to them – that this insanity is the reason so many firms cannot compete.

They're crippled and often killed *by their own conversations.*

Crafting and conducting a strategic conversation is a communications challenge. So framing is the one management tool every leader needs to be acutely conscious of, and to deliberately apply at every opportunity. It is, after all, what communication is all about, and what makes society and its institutions – including companies – what they are.

PRINCIPLE #3:
Keep your purpose simple

Every business, like every human being, needs a reason to exist – a "hill" to aim for. This gives them context, direction, and an overarching goal, to guide and inspire them.

Vision and mission statements are meant to do the job. Some firms have swung to "strategic intent," a term that has been around since Gary Hamel and C.K. Prahalad invented it in 1989.[7] And now "purpose" is gaining favour.[8] So we have four notions that capture the essence of what a business is up to, and it's not unusual for managers to use them all, depending on what pops into their minds.

Even when firms are consistent, few of them use any of these "tools" well. Managers lose sight of why they're necessary. Instead of being specific about where they want to go, and what they will and will not do, they waste their time on flowery prose that says nothing. Their first and possibly most crucial decisions fail to inform the goals and activities that follow. Without a compass, their people flail about and do their own thing, oblivious to the greater good. And as it becomes increasingly impossible to align them, controls have to be tightened and even the smallest decisions have to be delegated upwards.

When CEOs brief me ahead of a strategy project, they almost always tell me, "We need to revisit our vision and mission." But more often than not they can't remember what these say – and when I talk to their colleagues, it turns out that none of them can either. It's the same in my business school classes, where 20 or 30 senior executives from a variety of big companies have no idea what's in their own statements. (And these are often the very people who so enthusiastically crafted that guff!)

You have only to suffer through one or two strategy sessions where senior executives argue about the precise wording in vision or mission statements, to understand just how hard it is to create shared meaning. "Excellent," "the leader," and "world class" can be interpreted in countless ways. Companies inevitably fall back on the same words – service, innovation, integrity, responsibility, accountability, professionalism ... yakkety-yak – for added gravity and excitement, but these also mean different things to different people, and are forgotten before the ink dries.

Debating whether to declare that shareholders rank above customers, or to put employees above everyone, can waste a ridiculous amount of time. Even worse are tortuous arguments about whether to insert a comma or a full stop in a sentence, or whether to call your employees "associates" or "colleagues."

To help clients deal with this muddle, I remind them why they need any statement at all, and I suggest they stick with *purpose.* It is, after all, what vision, mission, or strategic intent is about. I also warn them that what they wind up with will only be useful if they ruthlessly edit their thoughts, and express them in language that people will understand.

There are four questions to consider:

1. **Who do you serve?** Who is your "right" customer? What other stakeholders must you satisfy? What trade-offs are you willing to make between their various demands?
2. **What value do you deliver?** What do customers get from a

relationship with you? What is your "difference" and why does it matter?* What do you do for other stakeholders?

3. **How will you do it?** What should your business model look like?
4. **What is your ambition?** What do you want to achieve, and by when?[9]

When you draft your company's purpose, you might be tempted – or pushed – to say more than you need to. But it won't help to cobble together every thought you have about customers, your people, and saving the planet. Nor will it help to proclaim your goal to be No. 1, or "the leader," or the "most admired," without a clear explanation of what that means† and a convincing story about how you'll get there.

Go lightly, too, with boasts about your ethics and integrity, or your deep commitment to shared value, brands, the environment, equality, or diversity. Oh, and by the way, that you make superior profits too. And all this while you "have fun!"

Such beliefs and aspirations might be laudable, and you might indeed mean to give them serious attention. But they can't all be the reason your firm exists.

Besides, the more bloated your purpose becomes, the harder it will be for you to remember and communicate, and the less likely it will be to guide or inspire anyone.

---

* Rosser Reeves, a famous advertising pioneer, called this the unique selling proposition or USP, and there's no better definition (Rosser Reeves, *Reality in Advertising*, New York: MacGibbon and Key, 1961). Today, it's commonly termed a value proposition.

† Any of these could refer to various aspects of performance, from sales, market share, and profits, to quality, productivity, or innovation.

Your business purpose must signal immediately what you're about, so it must be clear, concise, and coherent. It must be worth signing up for. It must be believable. And it must lead logically to the activities that will bring it to life.

If it doesn't meet all these criteria, and if there's even a hint that you don't quite mean it, your uncertainty will infuse everything you do. The pressures you face to be everything to everybody will have you bouncing from one stakeholder agenda to another, and you'll satisfy no one.

One thing you shouldn't expect from your purpose is that its mere existence will unleash some hidden passion in your people, unite them in their efforts, and trigger unheard-of achievement. That has been the promise of visions and missions, and it has proved to be an empty one. The fervour with which "purpose" is bandied about suggests it holds some deeper spiritual meaning, and touches a deeper psychological need. The result shows up, too often, in soaring, fluffy language that equates better sales of baked beans with getting to Mars.

Your purpose serves a real and vital function. But only if you think it through rigorously, frame it tightly, and don't get carried away as a wordsmith.

PRINCIPLE #4:
Profit is paramount … but it's not everything

Organizations exist to create value for a range of stakeholders – all of whom think they should be first in the pecking order. However, it's impossible to treat them all equally. If you so much as hint to your people that you should do that, they'll be all over the place – and you know what'll happen to your ten bucks!

In the good old days, few people would argue with the assertion that the business of business was to make money for investors. But times are changing, and companies have to be attuned to the concerns and demands of other stakeholders. Issues such as climate change and inequality are making news, and themes such as customer well-being and service, community engagement, and gender and diversity have risen up management agendas.

The role of business as a social institution is a touchy issue. The problems of the world will ensure it's the subject of even hotter debate in future. Even as investor influence has shot up, an increasingly outspoken and empowered citizenry and intense media scrutiny have scared the hell out of companies. Powerful activists and movements like Greenpeace and Occupy This-Or-That can't be ignored. Political pressures and regulation force firms to override their selfish interests and behave differently than they might otherwise do. Codes of corporate governance lay ever more stress on a balanced approach to "people, planet, profit," and "sustainability reporting" is a very big deal.

Corporate social responsibility has become a major concern – not least among a new generation of employees. So business leaders have no choice but to proclaim their commitment to "doing well by doing good." And to walk their talk, because that may be the price of a licence to do business.

In 2010, *Harvard Business Review* began publishing a list of "The World's Best CEOs," based on a single objective measure: their total return to shareholders during their tenure. This changed in 2015, when an assessment of their companies' environmental, social, and governance (ESG) performance was included. But while such ratings will please many people, their usefulness as indicators depends on how success is defined and how attention to these matters will affect it.

Balanced scorecards are popular because they depict profit as just one measure among equals. But financial metrics remain the firm favourites. There's no getting away from the reality that businesses exist to produce profits – and this won't change. They're money machines. They may have many goals, but producing more money than they use is No. 1.

The simple reason is that if they fail at this they cannot fund their future. They cannot create employment or reward their people appropriately. Nor can they expand their operations, maintain or upgrade their resources, strengthen their capabilities, invest in innovation or marketing – or pay tax and enable government to do its job. Investors will abandon them. They will immobilize themselves.

So whatever else they set out to do – uplifting communities, aiding charities, sponsoring education or medical services, caring for the environment, assisting suppliers, developing products and services for bottom-of-the-pyramid customers – they do for their own financial advantage. There may be an element of altruism, of course. But when you get past the PR spin, money is always the prime motivator. With few exceptions, shareholder interests trump noble intentions.

Anyone who doubts this should note that aggressive fund managers and high-speed computer trading have caused the average time a share is held to fall dramatically – to about 200 days in the US, for example.[10] Or that when a new CEO rides to the rescue of a troubled company, there's likely to be a quick spike in its share price – and an equally sharp drop when he doesn't deliver.

Doing good is an increasingly necessary aspect of managers' jobs, but first they must make money for themselves and their investors.[11] Their careers and earnings depend on their ability to produce superior and sustainable profits.

No amount of public or political pressure will change this reality. Nor will it help any business leader to fudge definitions of sustainability or downplay their commitment to profit.

In his 20-year tenure as chairman of GE, Jack Welch's aggressive attitude to growth won him the title of "Neutron Jack," and his ability to ride economic cycles and deliver strong earnings year after year was legendary. According to a *Business Week* article in 1997, "he often was asked: 'How much more can be squeezed from the lemon?' His standard reply was that there is 'unlimited juice' to be had by gaining greater operating efficiencies."[12]

Yet in a 2009 *Financial Times* interview, he made an astonishing about-turn. "On the face of it," he said, "shareholder value is the dumbest idea in the world. Shareholder value is a result, not a strategy ... Your main constituencies are your employees, your customers and your products."[13]

If that shook managers, Michael Porter offers comfort. An economist himself, who has always pushed the primacy of profit, he has subtly adjusted his message in recent years.

In a 2006 *Harvard Business Review* article, "Strategy and Society," he and Mark Kramer advocated "a new way to look at the relationship between business and society that does not treat corporate success as a zero-sum game."[14]

And in a follow-up in 2011, they argued: "Businesses acting as businesses, not as charitable donors, are the most powerful forces for addressing the pressing issues we face.... The purpose of the corporation must be redefined as creating shared value, not just profit per se."[15]

On the face of it, these shifts are game-changers. But they're not all they seem to be.

Peter Drucker always saw profit as a result, not a goal, and wrote at length about the social responsibility of business. GE has always been mindful of its social impact, and even on Welch's watch, when it drew fire for various "social misdemeanours," such as refusing to clean up the Hudson River, it spent heavily on doing good elsewhere.

From careful reading of the articles by Porter and Kramer, it's clear that none of the firms they cite was prepared to forgo profit, or put anyone but shareholders first, in producing "shared value." Whether they cleaned up their processes, served poor people, enabled entrepreneurs, or assisted communities nearby their operations, it was because *there are opportunities to make money doing these things.* Or at least, because it helped them polish their marbles so they could continue making money from doing business as usual in all other respects.

The need to create shared value isn't a new one. But today it's more important than ever for everyone – and will become even more so. Not for some fanciful reason, and not just because business is a social citizen and does have social obligations, but because growth opportunities in traditional markets are dwindling, and this is the only way to connect with previously unserved or underserved markets.

Paradoxically, this means that making profits demands *more* attention, not less.

If the now popular term "inclusive strategy" is taken to mean that all a firm's stakeholders will gain equally by its existence, or that profit is anything but essential, business will be imperilled. If, on the other hand, it goads managers into asking, *"How can we serve all our stakeholders to make bigger profits?"* we'll all be better off.

You may be deeply uncomfortable with the notion of shareholder primacy. You may sincerely believe that business has a larger purpose, and that your company is there for the "greater good." You might be convinced that you should put your employees, a community, or your customers first, or that innovation should be your clarion call.

But think about it.

Think about the logic and the implications of whatever you decide. Ask: Will it get you *all* the results you seek? Will it get you the support you need? And will it apply through the inevitable business cycles that affect every firm?

Agreeing with Milton Friedman, another Nobel economics laureate, Robert Solow, says, "It's not the business of the individual manager to say, 'What would be good for the health of the economy?' It's primarily the business of the individual manager to increase efficiency and profitability."[16]

The choice is yours. For me, it's clear that profit comes first, though with due attention to the range of other factors that contribute to it. This should not be something to fudge or deny.

PRINCIPLE #5:
Excel in the basics, strive for breakthroughs

If there's one question that bedevils strategic thinking and gets strategists' knickers in a twist, it's this: *Should you start planning your future from where you are or from where you'd like to be?*

The answer is, you have to do bits of both.

Strategists have to manage the present and the future at the same time. They have to run today's business as well as possible, but with a sense of what tomorrow's business will be. So they must excel in the basics, while at the same time seeking breakthroughs that will lead to future success.

This is often described as trying to fly a plane while changing the engines and wings. But the analogy might be too simple. The real challenge might be akin to flying a plane while *inventing a new way to fly*. Or a new way to *travel*. Or a way to let customers experience the world, visit each other, or do business ... *without having to travel.*

This is all very exciting. But before you aim for the stratosphere, calm down and come back to earth.

Entrepreneurs like Jeff Bezos and Elon Musk, or Larry Page and Sergei Brin, are thrilling to watch. There's apparently no limit to their imagination or ambition. Or their willingness to lay huge bets for the future.

But in these respects, they and their companies are outliers.

Most executives aren't cut from the same cloth, and most firms aren't anything like Amazon, Tesla, or Google – and never will be. So while they should inspire us all, we need to take note of what enables them to do what they do.

Those three companies are where they are not just because of their founders' vision, but because those rare individuals have built and run exceptionally effective organizations. They attract, satisfy, and retain talented staff and valuable customers. They improve and innovate relentlessly. Their operations hum.

Having put in place the foundations for growth, they're able to keep finding new opportunities for growth. As masters of the mundane, they're perfectly positioned to soar.

The logic in this is clear, but may not be what CEOs want to hear when they call me to talk strategy. Even if they see the need to review or fine-tune what they're already doing, they almost always hope for more radical action. They want dramatic leaps rather than "mere" improvement.

Yet in most cases, when I learn more about their firms, it becomes clear that a "moonshot" is not the first thing they should aim for.

What almost all of them should do, as a priority, is get their basics right – or, as I tell them, *"Fill the tank and pump the tyres!"*

Here are more reasons why:

First, there are often huge untapped opportunities right under managers' noses, yet they blithely leave money on the table while they chase after "a better way." They get distracted from fixing what's broken or not working, and wringing every last drop of sales and profit from their current business. Or they pursue new growth through acquisitions, despite evidence that *organic* growth is usually more profitable.

Second, finding novel ways to do business is no easy matter. It requires resources and concerted effort and seldom happens overnight. And since bold bets mostly don't pay off, it's extremely risky.

Third, any organizational change brings stress, so if a firm's foundations aren't sound, seemingly insignificant changes in one area can massively disrupt activities elsewhere. Extreme changes are far more serious. Reinventing strategy – especially if that triggers a raft of changes in one go – is sure to throw everything out of whack. The trauma can be too much for a system to withstand.

Fourth, managers who can't get today's business working properly are unlikely to do better trying to invent and run something totally new. If they're unable to make the most of what they've got, there's no reason to back them when they gamble on the unknown. With more balls in the air, they'll inevitably become less, not more, effective.

But that's not all.

Another factor that few people acknowledge, but that casts a long shadow over these four, is this:

Every business is to some extent a prisoner of its context, and bound by the rules of whatever game it plays. Bucking the system might sound like the best way out, but it may not be sensible or even possible. There's a time and a place for everything, and pushing for a first-mover advantage can be fatal.

For all the noise about traditional industry definitions having given way to new notions of "market space," and despite the hullabaloo about "strategic degrees of freedom," "blue oceans," and "thinking out of the box," most companies have less freedom than they imagine to rewrite the rules of their game.

As markets mature, competitors develop an understanding of what it takes to play, and come to a "dominant logic" which causes them all to do roughly the same things in roughly the same ways, and their offerings to converge.

When Lou Gerstner took on the challenge of turning IBM

around in the early 1990s, he came under intense pressure to break up "Big Blue," as the giant firm was known, and change direction. But he refused, saying,

> It is extremely difficult to develop a unique strategy for a company; and if the strategy is truly different from what others in the industry are doing, it is probably highly risky. The reason for this is that industries are defined and bounded by economic models, explicit customer expectations, and competitive structures that are known to all and impossible to change in a short period of time.[17]

This is why banks behave in many ways like other banks, steel companies like steel companies, and oil companies like oil companies. One fast-food chain might sell chicken while another sells burgers, but their underlying operations are much the same. A manufacturer of jam doesn't have infinite options when it comes to what ingredients to use, how to make the product, or how to distribute it. Nor can it act like a business selling motorbikes or insurance. Sure, there may be lessons from other industries, and some of their practices might be useful, but there are limiting factors too. And the jam maker's direct competitors are equally constrained by them.

But it's not just the factors cited by Gerstner that get in the way of innovation.

Conformity is imposed by regulation, and facilitated and accelerated by the rapid adoption of common management practices, the global diffusion of information and technology, and the ready availability of services and finance. Many companies that compete furiously also rely on the same suppliers and distributors.

In big or growing markets, this may not matter too much;

there's room for lots of players – at least for a while. But inevitably, as competitors race down the same path, they start falling over each other. Before they know it, customers can't tell them apart.

In highly regulated industries, there may be few options. In less-regulated ones, bruising price wars are sure to erupt.[18]

So what to do next?

You and your team might be turned on by throwing caution to the wind and beginning your strategic conversation with visioning and "backcasting."* Or you may set up innovation teams to plot "a new journey" that will take you to a happy future. But you can't wish current reality away. You are where you are and the sector you compete in is what it is.

Notions of "getting back to basics" and "key factors of success" (KFS) have been around for decades. And although innovation junkies may sniff at them, and you may hear about them less often than in the past, they're as relevant today as ever.

Most companies will almost certainly improve their results and widen their advantage if they clearly understand the rules of the game they play, and the key factors of success in that game, and then excel in both those and the critical core. Yet it's remarkable how many fall down on the small stuff.

They make promises they apparently never intend to keep. Their offerings aren't all they're cracked up to be, and come with conditions and catches. They make it hard for customers to buy from them, and force them into fights over service. Deliveries are late. Spare parts are unavailable. Administrative botch-ups create endless frustration.

---

* Thinking back from the future.

By now, doing the right things, the right way, on time, the first time and every time, should be normal. In fact, it's nowhere close.

What an opportunity!

What are "the basics" in your business?

On its own, of course, brilliance in the basics won't lead to lasting advantage. Even if you're able to keep *improving* for a long time, so will your competitors. Without *innovation*, your competitive edge will erode. And in today's hostile environment, new ideas come along at a blistering pace.

So breakthroughs are imperative.

In a comment on his book *Giants of Enterprise*, a study of seven famous business leaders, Harvard historian Richard Tedlow observes that they "all stood for something in their company, in their industry, and in society. In addition, they all had a *searing insight* they were able to communicate clearly and concisely to others – like Henry Ford's observation at the beginning of the 20th century that what people in the country needed was an inexpensive automobile."[19] (My italics.)

Do you have a "searing insight" about your business – and if so, what is it? What do you see in your environment, your industry, your market, your customers that no one else sees? What is your purpose, and what *could* it be? What difference do you make, and why does it matter? What difference *could* you make – and why would that matter? What might you offer that no one else has imagined?

You need to put yourself in the shoes of various stakeholders when you think about these questions, but the obvious place to start is with customers. Imagine what life is like for them. What are their needs, wants, worries, ambitions? What value are they getting from you and others today? What value might they want in future? How well are you satisfying them now, and how could you change? What will that require from your organization, and what operational changes could you make that would set you apart? How feasible is any of this *for you*? Is there money in it? How will competitors respond?

And what about *non*-customers? Who are they? What is value to them, and who provides it? Why don't they buy from you? How might you attract them? Would that be worthwhile? Can you do it? How will chasing them affect your current business?

What's your "searing insight"?

All this presents you with a tricky juggling act.

Managing the present and the future at the same time requires masterful orchestration of your strategic conversation. People must be kept mindful of the constraints they face in a particular market, and of the need to keep honing the basics, even while they're encouraged to break loose and explore new possibilities. They must focus on the here and now, but also imagine ways not just to defy or rewrite the rules of the game but to change the game altogether. And resources – *that darned Ten-Buck Test again!* – must be allocated in ways that make possible results in both the present and the future.

You can't do any of this in a vacuum. Having a clear purpose will ensure that you have direction and don't zigzag all over the place. You must also know what you'll do to get from here to there (Figure 2.2).[20] As I'll show in the next chapter, tight timelines and rapid action will help you bridge the gap between the present and the future in a way that lets you make the most of today's business while also moving relentlessly towards the business of tomorrow.

Figure 2.2

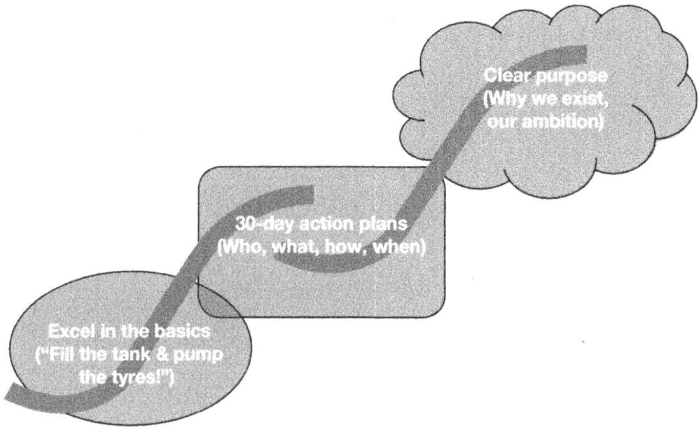
Clear purpose
(Why we exist,
our ambition)
30-day action plans
(Who, what, how, when)
Excel in the basics
("Fill the tank & pump
the tyres!")

PRINCIPLE #6:
Action is the goal

To emphasize their bold, overarching, and long-term intentions, nations and armies have a long tradition of packaging them as "grand strategy." This is stirring stuff, so management thinkers were bound to follow suit.

In an early definition of corporate strategy, Harvard Business School professor Kenneth Andrews said this:

> Corporate strategy is the pattern of decisions in a company that determines and reveals its objectives, purposes, or goals, produces the principal policies and plans for achieving those goals, and defines the range of businesses the company is to pursue, the kind of economic and human organization it is or intends to be, and the nature of the economic or noneconomic contribution it intends to make to its shareholders, employees, customers, and communities.

Business strategy, he said – or what would now be termed *competitive* strategy – is "less comprehensive [and] defines the choice of product or service and market of individual businesses within the firm."[21]

Andrews and his HBS cohort saw the ultimate purpose of all strategy as the achievement of organizational goals, which obviously required that specific *actions* be taken. But their emphasis was on *decisions and choices* – and they went so far as to label their subject "business *policy*."

This, and the virtually universal belief at the time in top-down control, led legions of managers to think of strategy as a high-level view of how a firm should go about its business; and to wallow in platitudes and vagueness while giving short shrift to *activities* and *action*. If they were responsible for choosing where and how to compete, the nitty-gritty of making and selling stuff was for lesser mortals. Micro-management became a pejorative term, and being branded a micro-manager plainly marked you as not being a leader.

The "vision, mission, values" gang continues in this tradition, as sure as ever that lofty notions and fine intentions will bring the results they want amid the scrum of hypercompetition. But as it has become increasingly apparent that strategy is only as sound as the activities that flow from it, and that turning strategy into action is finally what counts and always a challenge, smart managers have come to realize two things:

First, *no amount of analysing and planning will on their own bring success*. For that, you need to do different things than your competitors, or do the same things differently.[22]

You have to choose what to do, and also what *not* to do; and make hard trade-offs to get to the few activities that will make the biggest difference. And whatever you settle on must be followed by continual improvement and innovation – and excellence in execution.

Second, *strategy is a learning process*. It unfolds in a dynamic and unpredictable world. You have to make commitments, but they're for a future you can't quite see. So the best you can do is face up to that risk, mitigate it however you can, and then act, learn, and adjust as fast as possible.*

The past three or four decades have thus seen a distinct shift in thinking about strategy – at least by some people.

* This was the theme of my book *The Race to Learn* (Cape Town: Juta & Co., 1991). The need for speed is now even more imperative.

Whereas once it was considered to be an intellectual undertaking, all about weighty decisions and quite separate from the messy business of doing actual work, now the line is blurred.

Whereas once it was assumed that the future would be much like the past, and strategy could and should be designed to roll out predictably over multiple years, it's acknowledged today that even the most carefully crafted strategy can unravel in weeks or days.

So if ever there was merit in niggling about the difference between strategy and tactics, or about the relative importance of strategy and operational excellence, that time is long gone. Such hoary debates slow things down just when they need to be speeded up.

Strategy is not a desk job. Strategic thinking guides action, but learning through action is the only way to keep strategy relevant and effective.

The famous Tom Peters battle cry to "Try lots of stuff" is just what many companies need to hear. "Ready, fire, aim" goes down a treat in management conferences, and Nike's "Just Do It" has been filched by any number of managers keen to show their mojo.

But compelling as the need may be for experiments, action, and bureaucracy busting, just being busy won't make any company competitive.

Action without *reason* is likelier to bring costs and risks than positive results.

Action that doesn't lead to useful learning is wasted opportunity.

Studies by McKinsey Global Institute have shown that in the same industry across countries there are "almost always dramatic differences in either labor productivity or total factor productivity."

These differences, says Robert Solow, who has long served as academic advisor to MGI, are explained not by differences in technology or investment, but rather by "organizational differences, to the way tasks were allocated within a firm or division – essentially to failures in management decisions."[23]

For strategy to be effective, it must be *specific*, not only about high-level aims, but also about the actions that will occupy low-level people. Anything less is just hot air.

- Fred Gluck, founder of McKinsey's strategy practice, made a point of this in a 1979 paper he drafted for the consulting firm's staff, in which he advised that strategic planning should result in an "integrated set of actions designed to create a sustainable advantage over competitors."[24]
- According to UCLA professor Richard Rumelt, "Strategy is a way through a difficulty, an approach to overcoming an obstacle, a response to a challenge." The cleverest strategies, "the ones we study down through the years, begin with very few strategic resources, obtaining their results through the adroit coordination of actions in time and across functions."[25]
- Michael Porter writes that the primary purpose of a strategy is "to inform each of the thousands of things that get done every day, and to ensure that those things are all aligned in the same direction."[26]
- And Eric Van den Steen, a member of the HBS Strategy Unit, provides the best definition of strategy I know of, saying it's "the smallest set of choices and decisions sufficient to guide all other choices and decisions."[27]

All these experts make it plain that strategy is not an end in itself, but rather a means to getting the right things done in the right way. None of the four suggests it's the work of managers to precisely translate activities into actions, or get down in the weeds and mess with every minor decision, or meddle in every activity. Nor does any of them suggest you should be the doer-in-chief, with *everybody's* to-do list sitting on your desk in a detailed master list. You have neither the time nor the energy for all this, and attempting it will demotivate your people and make your organization weak and dysfunctional.

What Gluck, Rumelt, Porter, and Van den Steen do say is that *your job is to provide an overarching view of where and how you'll compete, and oversee the process of identifying and coordinating the actions that will produce the results you want. It's to craft and conduct the strategic conversation that will enable your people to be effective.*

Not surprisingly, many managers interpret this advice to suit their own inclinations. Struggling to wring profits from strategies that ape those of their competitors, and unable to innovate, they rely on execution to differentiate themselves. And they're encouraged in this by a sharp rise in the number of books, articles, courses, and conferences on the topic, many of which point to the need for intense, hands-on involvement in operational matters. The result is that management based on purpose, inclusion, and trust has given way to getting down and dirty in the trenches with the troops. And that micro-management is alive and well in many firms – though practised under the cloak of empowerment, "leaderless teams," self-organization," and other fashionable notions.

There's a lot to be said for the "loose-tight" approach identified by Peters and Waterman in *In Search of Excellence.*[28] Managers have everything to gain by being more overt about it, and everything to lose by pretending that loose is good and tight is bad – or tight is good and loose is bad.

The dilemma, as with so much else, is how to strike the balance.

PRINCIPLE #7:
Strategy, leadership, and change management are inextricably linked by a single seamless conversation

Strategy doesn't have a neat beginning and end. Creating strategy and executing it can't be cleanly separated. Insights, decisions, and action are woven together in an intricate and messy process.

All firms have to cope with an incessant barrage of external and internal changes. They make no progress if they keep doing what they were doing, the way they always did it. Or if they apply a tweak here and a tweak there from time to time. Nor will they get where they want to go if they just mooch along and react to whatever comes at them. They survive and thrive only if they proactively and deliberately act in new and different ways to improve and innovate.

The whole point of strategy is change. That must always be the outcome.[29]

This might mean that you adopt an incremental approach and strive for more, better, faster, and cheaper. Or it could demand something radical – "shock and awe." Or a combination of both.

Whichever it is, all strategic conversation should challenge people's assumptions, encourage possibility thinking, and facilitate the development of confidence and competence across an organization. At the same time, it must highlight new priorities, trigger new action, and make new beliefs, methods, and routines "the way we do things around here."

Continuous change must be made normal and natural – a taken-for-granted yet also top-of-mind aspect of everyday work.

This is what makes a firm fast, flexible, and resilient, and makes the future a matter of choice, not chance.

If this is true, then *surely managers should strive for excellence in both strategy and change management – and use their strategic conversation to facilitate both at the same time.*

But few seem to get this.

It's highly unusual to walk into a workplace where there's *no* change management project under way. Almost any excuse for one will do. So there's a proliferation of meetings, workshops, training sessions, presentations, personal counselling, and so on, all intended to change something or other. This is astonishing, given how costly and distracting – and often utterly inappropriate – this "busy-work" is. And even more so given that change management interventions have a terrible record, with study after study showing that *around three-quarters of them don't deliver the expected results.*

The fact is, they're largely a waste of time – perhaps even useless!

There are many reasons for this dismal outcome. "This needs some change management" cannot possibly be the right fix for everything; but it's trotted out at the drop of a hat to deal with just about anything. Then, the approach that's chosen might not be the best one. Or the environment might not be supportive. Or sponsors of "the project" might lose interest. Or other matters crop up and drag things off course.

At the top of the list, though, is the fact that change efforts are typically left to consultants or HR folk, and not led by the line managers whose role it is to get results from their people. And however competent such advisors might be, they lack the managers' clout and won't be around when they're needed.

It's not their job to craft and conduct the strategic conversation. They do not directly shape the climate in which people work. Nor can they be held accountable for coaching and mentoring, guiding and inspiring, or providing the rapid feedback and frequent praise that people need.

Instead of seeing change management as an integral aspect of strategy, essential in giving it life, and thus one of their most important responsibilities, managers too often treat it as a Band-Aid, and a nuisance they can safely assign to someone else. They get high on strategy, draft detailed plans, and toss them over the wall to others who'll hopefully drive whatever changes are needed. And they wonder why their brilliant strategies grind to a halt and gather dust.

There are any number of change management models and methods. But as I pointed out in my first book, *Communicating for Change* (Juta, 1987), the process essentially involves four steps. You could add more in between these, and flesh out the detail, but here are the basics:

1. Create dissatisfaction with the status quo.
2. Debate possible futures.
3. Act to learn.
4. Review and revise (Figure 2.3).[30]

Now, if you think about it, exactly the same process applies to strategy (more on this on pages 116–120). And because strategy and change management hold equal sway in getting a firm to a different place, dealing with them sequentially makes no sense. Far better that you see them as one, and begin with change management when you start work on your strategy.

Figure 2.3

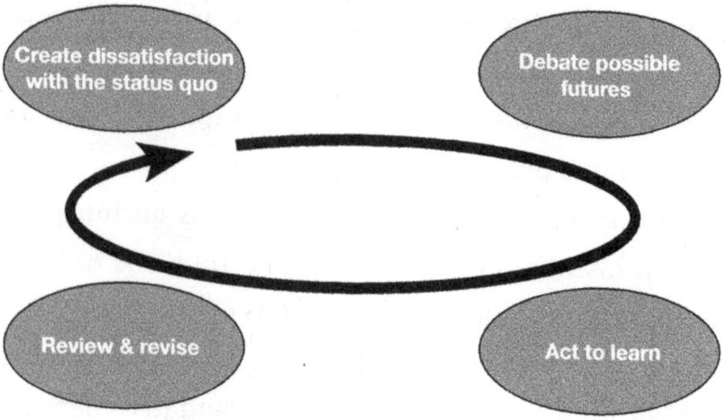

Efforts to bring about change usually begin and end with trying to change people's minds in hope that they'll then change their behaviour. That's not easy to do, and it seldom works.

For one thing, a cause with more conscripts than volunteers has little chance of success. Sometimes you do have to call the shots and tell people what must change, and how. But it's almost always better to involve them in deciding it's necessary, and what approach will work best.

Secondly, there's plenty of evidence that people are more likely to change their minds as a result of changing their behaviours than the other way around. Getting them to *do* new things is the surest way to get them to *think and believe* new things. And it's reason to strive for action as fast as possible!

Leaders are expected to have clear opinions about what needs to change about their organizations, and how. And it's tempting, when they're under pressure for results, for them to issue orders and avoid long debates. But as MIT professor Edgar Schein and many other experts in change confirm – and as my simple model shows – the best results usually come from involving as many people as possible, as early as possible and continually, in sensing the need for change and in deciding what must change, and why, how, and when that must happen.

Sharing responsibility this way means they create their own case for change, so you don't have to convince them. It means that having thought about a situation themselves, they'll be more open to considering new ways to address it, and acting on them. And that when they then reflect on the results, they'll be likely to say, "So far so good, but there's more to do" – so the cycle becomes self-perpetuating.

The emphasis from the start and throughout is on action. On encouraging people to contribute their own ideas, find their own solutions, and own what must follow; on enabling them to practise new behaviours and embed new habits, and to learn by doing; and on using their successes to build confidence and competence and encourage further progress.

The four-step process is a multi-purpose tool that applies as much to wrenching, company-wide "strategic" change as it does to lesser problems such as moving office, shifting to flexitime, bringing in new technology, or introducing a new procurement system. And it applies equally to any effort to scale up a business or to ramp up innovation, quality, or productivity. This doesn't mean you have to make a huge thing of it for every little challenge, but you should at least have it in mind.

Of course, change may demand new organizational arrangements such as facilities and equipment, HR policies, recruitment or restructuring, promotions, pay, and incentives. And, yes, it may be helped along by the judicious use of internal communications or training programmes, or by a new corporate identity or advertising campaign.

But what really triggers and sustains it is a *new strategic conversation.*

As we've seen, companies cannot fulfil their purpose while treating strategy and change management as discrete functions to be worked at separately, at different times, and probably by different people. But whatever difficulties they create for themselves by persisting in this mode are made worse if they also think of *leadership* as a separate matter (Figure 2.4).[31]

Figure 2.4

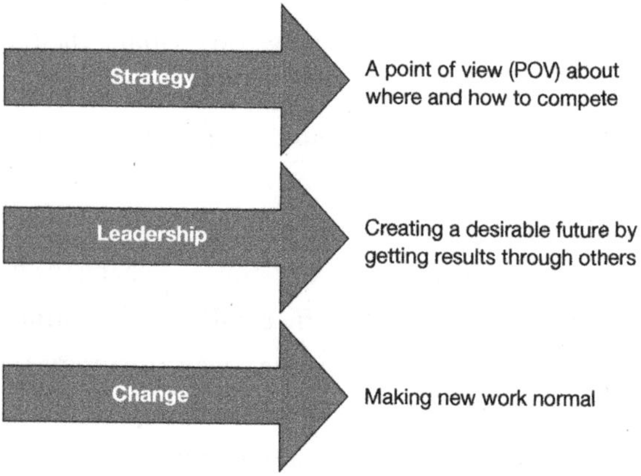

This flawed yet pervasive paradigm leads to unnecessary work and costs, destroys agility, and is a significant cause of poor performance. It's an obsolete view that serves no one. Yet it's what the management advice industry teaches and preaches, despite a growing amount of evidence against it.

The result is that strategy-making in organizations goes something like this:

"We need a new strategy."
"That's done. Now we have to change to make it work."
"Right. So that will require leadership. Who will it be?"

The time to start thinking about how you'll turn your intentions into action is when you start thinking about where and how to compete – or maybe even before that. And when you start working your plan, you should be thinking about how you'll change it when you need to.

Strategy cannot be cast in stone. Change management cannot be of occasional concern. But nor is leadership a panacea to be invoked from time to time, or to help processes that are already under way. Our VUCA environment changes constantly and in surprising ways, and you have to keep adjusting to it. Someone has to lead all the way.

The change cycle makes it glaringly obvious that leadership, strategy, and change management are inextricably connected in one seamless, continuous cycle (Figure 2.5). Each affects the others, and is affected by them. It makes no sense to deal with any of them in isolation – and doing so is sure to hamper performance.[32]

Figure 2.5

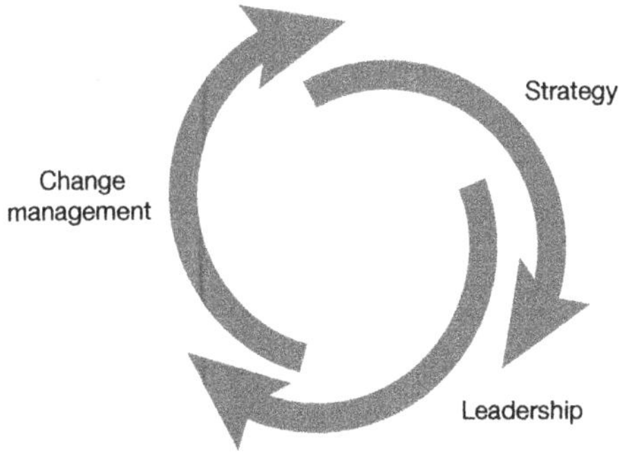

Strategic conversation is the common thread in each of these functions.

Growth leadership is the first of the eight critical strategy practices, and for good reason. The other seven practices all require context, direction, and support, and must be monitored and fine-tuned. And while each of them necessarily involves specific discussion, a company's overarching strategic conversation is what enables them to function as a system.

But let's drill down further.

Leadership at every level of an organization is a prerequisite for success, and different things need to be spoken about at head office, say, than in a marketing or production meeting. But local, operational matters must always be considered within an overall context, which means they are logically framed by the strategic conversation.

An executive in charge of a new product initiative, for example, will address matters such as customer insight, design, prototype testing, and supply chain arrangements – while always considering the company strategy. The head of HR is expected to draft sensible recruitment policies, deal with unions, and offer sound training programmes – but again, to suit the strategy. And the same will happen in every other functional area.

So here's the paradigm of the future:

Leaders must be both strategists and change managers.

Strategists need leadership and change management skills to get results.

Change management begins when you make strategy, and is contingent on leadership.

Strategic conversation is the one tool that links all three functions and makes them effective.

PRINCIPLE #8:
Culture matters – and climate, not engagement, is a key factor in managing it

One aspect of organizational life that's a perennial target for change management is culture. And it's easy to see why.

For one thing, it affects everything companies do and the way they do everything. That old saw that culture trumps strategy is true; culture must align with strategy and support it, or it'll suck the life out of even the best of intentions.

Second, adapting culture to an ever-changing context is essential to meeting strategic goals, so it's a key aspect of managerial work. This job is never done.

And third, culture is a reflection of human assumptions, beliefs, values, and behaviours – the soft "people stuff" that's such fun to meddle with.

But let's look at what culture is, why it exists, and why so many attempts to change it go wrong.

A simple analogy helps explain:

An imaginary "tape recorder" in our brains records our lives – the sights, sounds, smells, touches, and other experiences that merge into a point of view* about what's best for us. Then, whenever we face a new challenge, we replay that tape to see if there's anything on it that'll help us deal with what's ahead. So our past informs our future. Whether we realize it or not, we're effectively prisoners of our experience, both guided and constrained by "what we know."

---

* Also known as a mindset, world view, paradigm, or mental model.

This is as true for individuals as for groups (though with groups we're talking about a *collective* record of the past). Our life stories frame what we see and how we make sense of it; a company's history does the same.[33]

Memory is a product of experience, and culture is a product of memory. Culture is defined by our past, and in turn prescribes how we act now and in the future. Thus it's both a *consequence* and a *cause.*

Because it's not easy to wipe away either personal or organizational memories, and it takes time for new ones to take hold, culture is extremely "sticky." Also, it's as subject to path dependence as any other resource.[34] So, as an imprint of everything we do and the way we do everything is laid down on our mental tape recordings, "lock-in" occurs and makes it much easier to keep doing what we've always done rather than change course.

Now let's say you need your employees to consistently deliver knockout customer service. How would you get them to do this? How, in other words, would you change the culture to make such service normal?

Begin with what Edgar Schein told me in an interview:

> You change people's behaviour, and you may eventually influence their beliefs. If you define culture as a common learned response, then it changes with success. Change comes from success, not from somebody imposing something new.
>
> When people ask me to diagnose or change culture, my first question always is, "Why?" And, "What problem are you facing that makes you want to change anything?" You need to force them to be clear about the business problem or organ-

izational problem that's motivating any change. And then the culture comes in.[35]

Now, apply that thinking in your workplace.

If employees are to consistently deliver great customer service, they need some reason to accept that it makes sense to do so. Then, as they act on this assumption, they accumulate memories of what they did and how customers responded – which hopefully confirms they're on the right track, strengthens their commitment, and leads them to repeat the new behaviour. Through a process of practice and reflection, they develop a service habit, and a service culture gradually takes hold.

The same approach applies where, for example, cost control, quality, innovation, or excellent execution are company goals. Visible and vocal leadership can get things going, but *real change only begins when people start to act in new ways.*

This is an ongoing task, not one you can pull off in a few workshops, or maybe not even in just a few months. And it's definitely not one that can be left to some consultant or to HR. It has to be right at the top of the *leader's* agenda.

Culture change is hard work. Breaking old habits and developing new ones takes time. But even if you're in a hurry to make a difference, you'll do well to bolster your use of the *action* lever with use of another one: *your organization's climate.*

Although the concept of organizational climate has been around since the 1930s, there's surprisingly little mention of it in the management literature. This despite the fact that measuring it remains a widespread practice, and executives still refer to "climate studies" when discussing how their people feel.

So what is it, exactly? How does it relate to the currently fashionable notion of *engagement*? And why should you care?

According to my *Oxford English Dictionary*, *climate* is a noun referring to weather conditions. *Engage* is a verb meaning "to occupy, attract, or involve." So logically, a firm's climate – or "weather" – is the set of conditions that determine how people feel at work, and thus how engaged they'll be.*

Climate is determined by the bundle of organizational factors that enable and encourage positive results.

First come *sound working conditions* – facilities, communication, role clarity, resources, support, policies, rewards, etc. These are the bedrock, which is why they're called *hygiene* factors. They're also an easy target for action by HR, who can directly influence changes in them. (In the scheme of things, however, their positive impact may be much less than the dissatisfaction that arises when they're not attended to.)

The bigger issue is people's perceptions and feelings. Not just about their working environment, but, more importantly, about themselves.

These are most powerfully influenced by the overall *management approach*, which is expressed through respect, trust, involvement, challenges, decision rights, recognition, feedback, and opportunities for growth.

All of these are *inputs*, which management can influence. And when effectively combined, they give people a sense of *purpose* and *meaning*, which are the ultimate motivators.

---

* If surveys to assess climate and engagement in an organization are to be effective, they should obviously measure different things; in fact, they often overlap.

Engagement, on the other hand, is an *outcome* – a consequence of a firm's climate, a response to the environment. It's a reflection of people's commitment to their work; their motivation and willingness to go the extra mile; their interest in learning and improving their contribution; and perhaps – at a stretch – their loyalty to their employer.

Engagement, in other words, is an indicator of purpose and meaning.

This distinction between climate and engagement might seem like hair-splitting, but it matters enormously:

You can only change employee engagement levels by changing the climate.

So climate change has to be an early step in culture change!

You can't get away from the fact that although organizational climate has become an unfashionable concept, it remains a vital lever for change. In fact, as I'll show shortly, growth leadership (Critical Strategy Practice #1) is impossible without specific attention to climate.

PRINCIPLE #9:
Everyone needs strategic IQ

Every organizational activity relates to strategy in some way or other. Yet strategy continues to be seen as a specific function best left to a selected handful of senior executives, and few firms see the value in building strategic capabilities across a wide swathe of their people. Achieving this is seldom an explicit goal, and little effort is made to provide opportunities for it to happen.

To compete in a rapidly changing world, ever more companies need people who can see the big picture, make sense of what's happening around them, and make rapid and sound decisions about how to respond – not efficient drones who are oblivious to their environment, mindlessly take orders, and just do as they're told. The need is even greater due to the shift in much of the workforce towards educated and mobile millennials who are expected to be a font of new ideas.

Because so many of a firm's people might set off – or invent – a response to environmental changes, strategy is a task almost everyone is involved in. Yet while recruitment and development processes continue to emphasise *cognitive IQ* and *emotional IQ*, what's missing is almost any concern about *strategic IQ* – perhaps the most underrated capability in business.

So what exactly is this third form of intelligence? And how is it best developed?

Strategic IQ is the ability to think strategically, which in turn leads to the ability to act strategically. It's firstly an *individual* capability, but it also needs to be an *organizational* capability.

Think about it like this:

Assume you're about to hire a consultant to help you with your strategy. You obviously want the best strategy you can get. So what thinking skills would you expect of the person you're about to rely on?

Surely they'd be these:

- **Foresight** – the ability to see into the future, anticipate what lies ahead, and decipher what it means.
- **Insight** – the ability to cut through clutter and complexity and to understand things incisively and in a new way.
- **Analysis** – the ability to collect information, decipher and make sense of it, and make it useful.
- **Imagination** – the ability to see what others have not seen, and to think "what could be" where others are content with what is.
- **Synthesis** – the ability to connect disparate scraps of information, different sensations and perceptions, and unrelated ideas, so as to give them new meaning and make the whole greater than the sum of the parts.
- **Judgment** – the ability to weigh up situations, facts, feelings, opinions, and so on, and to make choices about what must be done in a way that best balances risk and reward and leads to the most desirable outcomes possible (Figure 2.6).

Now, if these are the traits you'd want in a consultant, what about the people on *your own team*? What thinking skills should you seek in them? What should you strive to develop in *them*? What do they need in order to fulfil their purpose in a VUCA world?

Answer: Exactly the same capabilities.

Like other forms of intelligence, strategic IQ is a product of both nature and nurture. It can be improved through courses, reading, and exposure to experts. Formal training in topics like

Figure 2.6

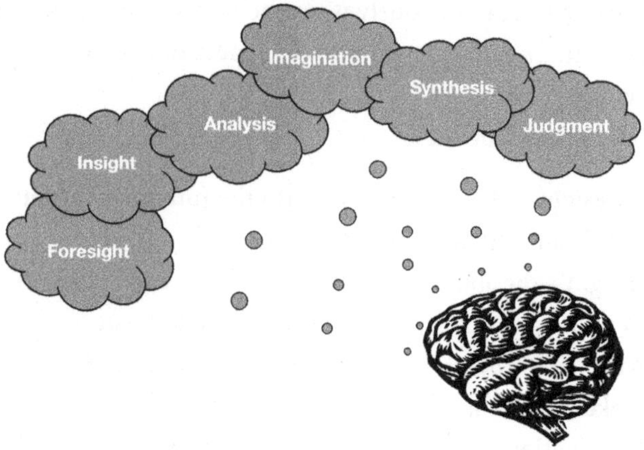

future and systems thinking, data analysis, and decision-making is helpful and should be available to more people than it is. But ultimately the only way to develop real competence is through deep immersion in strategy-making in the hurly-burly of the workplace. *Informal* development – real-world practice in making strategy – is more powerful than anything else.

Strategy is a learned skill. It's a slog. It requires knowledge, perspective, and wisdom that no amount of formal training can provide. Exposure to many situations is a prerequisite.

Without having soaked up information and experience, maybe over many years, and without actually "doing" strategy, few people can claim to be competent strategists. Just as you can't learn about soldiering from watching war movies, you can't learn about business strategy from the sidelines. You have to do it to "get it."

Studies of chess masters, and of exceptional performers in a wide variety of other fields, whether physical or mental, show that it takes about ten years of *deliberate practice and reflection* to become expert. This has led to the notion of "the ten-year rule" (also known as "the 10 000-hour rule").[36]

All capabilities, whether physical or mental, are developed in exactly the same way. It's an arduous process. But the payoff is that when crunch time comes – whether on the sports field, on a production line, or in a boardroom – instinct and intuition take over. "Gut feel" facilitates rapid and effective decisions and action.[37]

Obviously, not everyone can become a brilliant strategist. Nor does everyone need to, as most employees will never occupy "strategy" roles in their firms. But no matter what work they do, they'll undoubtedly be more effective in it if they're given the chance and the encouragement to learn as much as possible about strategy.

This will help them understand not only the *what* and the *how* of their jobs, but, perhaps even more important, *why* their inputs matter, thus giving them a sense of meaning and purpose. So they'll be better equipped and motivated to handle new challenges and assignments, and their companies will be better set to compete.

The strategic IQ of most organizations is pathetically low – not because of the way they make strategy, but because they don't deliberately strive to lift that IQ or take advantage of everyday work to do so.

You can change that fast, by immediately involving as many people as possible in your company's "big conversation." This single step will do more than anything else to align and energize your team, and empower them to conquer tomorrow.

PRINCIPLE #10: Acknowledge the need for balance in everything

We live in a world of tensions and paradoxes.

Success in business requires hard trade-offs and choices. And commitment. But it also demands compromise and balance.

We all admire strong people. Confidence in a leader is a vital trait, but overconfidence is a deadly flaw. Being able to develop a clear point of view is absolutely necessary, but sticking to it in the face of changing realities is downright stupid. To imagine that you're always right while everyone else is wrong is delusional.

There are two sides to every story. There's no "one best way" for most things, and "My way or the highway" is seldom the best route to success. There are times for this-*or*-that thinking, and times for this-*and*-that thinking.

Crafting a strategic conversation is about making initial decisions. *Conducting* it is about winning people's hearts and minds and inspiring their imagination and spirit – and about making new decisions, ensuring whatever might trigger new action becomes necessary, and winning continued support as events unfold.

Balance matters in both of these.

When you and your colleagues start work on your strategy, there are sure to be plenty of differences among you. Not everyone will agree on everything. People bring a lot of baggage to such discussions, and play games. (And they're especially prone to what Edward de Bono once called "face games" – meaning they're inclined to help others save face, even if it means lying to them!) So even if you conclude with what looks like consensus, they'll walk away with different opinions on the soundness of your strategy, and how seriously they'll back it. And you won't know. Nor will you necessarily know when they change their minds.

Your many other stakeholders also have their own world views, ambitions, and goals. They too will be less transparent than you'd like. And they too will keep changing their minds.

However much you strive to craft a perfect, *sustainable* strategy, you won't succeed; there is no such thing. No matter how much effort you put into nailing down your intentions, getting buy-in for them, or implementing them just as you planned, our VUCA world and shifting agendas will frustrate your best intentions. The strategy you put on the table will not survive being put into action.

Crafting and conducting strategy must be *synchronous*, not *sequential*, processes. "First this, then that" won't work. Every day brings the challenge, not only of dealing with the clutter on your desk or the ceaseless calls for your attention, but also reading the wind, deciding what can or cannot be priorities, starting some things and stopping others, siding with one point of view or another – all while pushing relentlessly forward.

No one said this would be easy. It's not work for wimps. You can't do it without being decisive. But nor can you do it without compromise and balance.

Keep that in mind and remind your team of it constantly.

Remind them too of all the ten principles you've read about here. For these are context for the critical core.

3

THE CRITICAL PRACTICES

Companies that do exceptionally well in the future will be those that excel in the basics of today, while also focusing intensely on the possibilities of tomorrow. They will be curious and adventurous, and driven to do more, better, faster – at ever-lower cost. They will bring us astonishing new products and services, delivered in ways we cannot yet imagine. And they will change the way we see the world, think of ourselves, and go about our lives.

These firms will work in a way that is informed by history, grounded in reality, and known to bring the best results. They will have a clear opinion on what it takes to compete and win, and will pursue bold goals through the imagination and spirit of their people. The eight critical strategy practices will be the core of their approach, and they will apply them resolutely and with discipline that borders on the fanatical.

Now, let's look more closely at those practices.

You might wish for long explanations about them, along with a full set of instructions for implementing them. But if I spell things out, you won't need to figure them out. And that's not the best start if you're to make ideas your own.

So I'm staying with my own mantra that less is more, and simpler is better.

I'll tell you why you need each of the practices, and how they add up logically to a powerful approach to management. And I'll suggest some of the issues and questions you need to consider in order to compete today and in the testing times that lie ahead. But the rest is up to you.

You'll get the most from these practices by reflecting on what you read here, thinking about them and talking about them with your team, and then deciding for yourselves how to apply them.

Learning by doing is the essence of the Harvard case-study

method, the Toyota Production System, and every successful approach to change management. As the adage says: "Give a man a fish, and you feed him for a day; show him how to fish, and you feed him for a lifetime."

Just as you don't need to keep scrabbling for new ideas in what Drucker so aptly called the "management gadget bag of techniques for the efficiency expert,"[1] neither do you need as much guidance as you might imagine to implement any of these practices.

There are no deep secrets here, only common sense. Having worked on all of the practices, with countless companies, I can assure you they're easy to understand and introduce without extensive hand-holding. Excelling in them will take serious and sustained effort, but if you keep reminding yourself *why* you need them, and persist in using them, you'll get what you want from them.

Let's begin with the real purpose of all concepts, tools, or techniques:

> *Every management idea is a framing device – and no more than that. All of them are based on particular assumptions about what leads to success. All that any of them does is promote and explain a particular approach to dealing with one issue or another, and encourage a certain way of talking about it. This, in turn, influences decisions and actions.*

On their own, management ideas do nothing. Until they provoke and shape conversations, they're worthless. For until that happens, they have no effect at all on behaviour – or results.

Balanced scorecards get managers talking about the range of performance measures most important to them. Michael Porter gets them talking about whether to pursue a "generic" strategy or one aimed at "differentiation," and how best to structure their "value chains" or "activity systems." Disruption theory invokes discussion about "sustaining" and "disrupting" innovation, "the job to be done," and "good enough" offerings. And the language of lean processes draws attention to doing things "right first time," and the elimination of costs and waste.

The eight practices comprising the critical core define what you and your colleagues must talk about, and hence what you'll pay attention to and where and how you'll apply your resources. Together, they're based on the fact that to be competitive every company must:

- Be led by people who are driven to grow their business, and to do it by growing their people.
- Learn what's happening in its world, and adapt, faster than rivals.
- Focus on making a difference that matters to specific customers, and continually deliver new and better value to them while also lowering costs.
- Design and create a sound business model – and change it when necessary.
- Get whatever resources and capabilities are called for, continually strengthen them, and use them to best effect.
- Develop and maintain sound relationships with stakeholders.
- Do things at the right time and speed.
- Be highly effective at execution.

Excellence in all of these requires that you *talk* about them – and not now and then, but constantly. And that you *act* on them. Only by doing this will they ever become habits, and add up to an unassailable advantage.

Along with the principles I described in the previous chapter, what follows will enable you to craft and conduct the strategic conversation you need now and in the future.

PRACTICE #1: Growth leadership

The first imperative for success is leaders at all levels with an unswerving commitment to growth, who live the tenet "*Grow the business by growing the people*" (Figure 3.1).

Figure 3.1

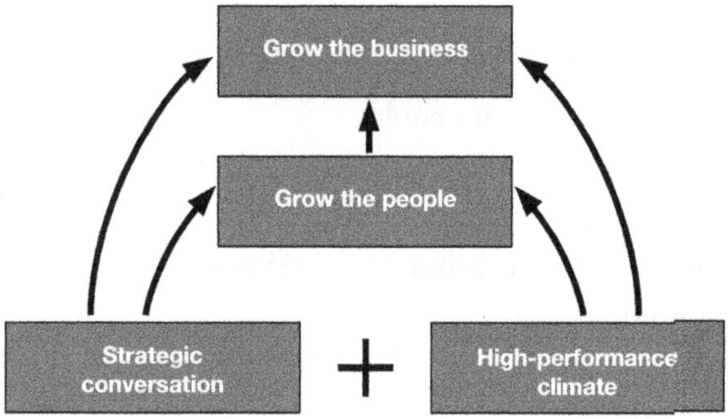

Growth – in sales and profits, as well as resources and capabilities – enables a company to survive in a hostile world, fund its future, and play a positive social role. If a firm doesn't get stronger, it will become weaker in relation to its competitors and less appealing to customers and investors; and other stakeholders may either shun it or take advantage of it.

So you may choose how much to grow, or how fast, but "grow or die" is a binary choice.

But make no mistake: business growth is neither natural nor normal. It doesn't come just because you turn up or make rousing speeches about it. Nor does it come though occasional surges in energy, or stabs at this or that. The fact is, it's an *aberration* – an out-of-the-ordinary product of ambition, courage, investment, innovation, and action; and also, with few exceptions, of luck. It invariably involves many setbacks and a great deal of discomfort.

Strangely, it's not unusual for senior executives to be ambivalent about growth. Or to express bold ambitions while failing to develop strategies or build organizations that have any chance of achieving them. But, in addition to these failings, their most common mistake is to not put their people front and centre of their strategies.

So the first and most important management practice – the one that provides context for all the others – has to be *an obsession with the growth of the business through the growth of its people.* On managing those people in a way that not only enables their delivery of intended business results, but also leads to their becoming more capable and confident.

Achieving both of these goals depends essentially on the same two levers that apply in changing culture:

The first is *strategic conversation*, because that crystallizes a firm's theory of success, and determines what gets attention and the actions that follow – and thus what people experience and learn. It also facilitates rapid adaptation.

Second is a *high-performance climate*, as that determines how people are able to work, and how they feel about doing it – which affects their motivation and thus facilitates exceptional effort and achievement.

Only by coupling an effective strategic conversation with a high-performance climate can you get the results you want.

Growth is born from the imagination and spirit of people, and results from both the fierce implementation of bold decisions and excellence in the small stuff. The single most valuable contribution of leaders is that they shape the conditions that foster it.

They must *want* growth, and be driven to seek the market and organizational opportunities that will make it possible. They must have a clear theory of success that provides direction and informs their strategic choices. And they must enable and inspire their people to perform at their best, to continually improve themselves, and always to push the bounds of possibility.

They do all this by framing the world for those around them through their words and actions – by crafting and conducting the conversations that are the seedbed of growth. So they must continually ask themselves:

1. What must our people *know* so they can do what they need to do?
2. How should they *feel* so they will do what they need to do?
3. What must *I* do to make it happen?

Of course, much else must be put in place, and we'll come to that shortly. But all depends on people. Nothing happens without them. Only if they volunteer insights and ideas, cooperation and effort, will a firm perform anywhere near its potential. They are either a limiting factor, or an engine of opportunity.

We all know this. There are no surprises here.

Except, perhaps, why so many companies persist in acting as if it were not true!

For the past 40-odd years, a furious leadership-vs-management debate has raged in management and academic circles. As a result, leading and managing have come to be generally seen as different types of work, performed by different types of people.

Managers deal with complexity, we're told. Leaders deal with change.[2] Or "Management is a bottom line focus: How can I best accomplish certain things? Leadership deals with the top line: What are the things I want to accomplish?"[3]

This is unquestionably one of the silliest notions in organizations today, and one of the most serious impediments to growth leadership. But the idea took hold – clearly with little thought to its flawed logic or implications.

However, by 1995, even Harvard professor John Kotter, long a champion of the "leaders and managers are different" view, had begun to temper his rigid opinion.

"Success in managerial jobs increasingly requires leadership, not just good management," he said. "Even at lower levels in firms, the inability to lead is hurting both corporate performance and individual careers. Organizations that stifle leadership from employees are no longer winning."[4]

Henry Mintzberg, one of the finest and most thoughtful management scholars around, puts it like this: "How would you like to be managed by someone who doesn't lead? That can be awfully dispiriting. Well, then, why would you want to be led by someone who doesn't manage? That can be terribly disengaging: how are such 'leaders' to know what is going on?"[5]

Those definitions "create a false dichotomy," says Harvard professor Jay Lorsch; "... the most effective leaders turn out to be very good managers as well ... if the only way to be a leader is to be bringing about change, there are an awful lot of us who think we are leading others when according to this dichotomy we are not."[6]

There's no point at all in blathering on about non-existent or insignificant differences between management and leadership. There's nothing to be gained – and much to be lost – by continuing to moan that organizations are over-managed and under-led. Nor are we helped by the many books and articles that bang on about this divide, the gurus who make a big thing of it, or the widespread emphasis on it in business schools.

The belief that managers and leaders are different species of quite different stature, with different roles and responsibilities, is sharply at odds with the necessity *for them to be at one in crafting and conducting a single, seamless conversation.*

What's more, it is generally accepted that leadership is about *creating a desirable future by getting results through others.* This focuses attention on five tasks:

1. Deciding what a "desirable future" might be.
2. Deciding what results are needed to get there, and how to achieve them.
3. Gaining the backing of key stakeholders.
4. Providing the necessary information, resources, and support.
5. Overseeing the activities that deliver the intended results.

Clearly, this is the work of anyone who goes by the title of either manager or leader. It requires them to inspire a sense of purpose, encourage people to volunteer their imagination and spirit and push their own limits, and ensure that necessary activities are properly carried out.

Firms do need structure and clear reporting lines. Everyone can't have the same authority to make every decision. But the fact that some people have to spend much of their time determining where next to expand, dealing with external stakeholders, or negotiating M&A deals, while others focus more on functional matters, does not justify ill-founded designations whose main impact on performance might be negative. Both groups are simultaneously leaders *and* managers (or simply *executives*). Both have a hand in growing the business by growing the people.

Both HR and the executives they support need to constantly remind themselves of the adage "Nothing succeeds like success." They need to ensure that they do whatever it takes to keep satisfaction levels high, and put the same effort into the practical measures that enable high performance.

Fortunately, says education expert Malcolm Knowles, "An organization provides an environment for adult education, an environment that either facilitates or inhibits learning."[7]

Companies are classrooms. They're where people learn most of their business skills. Yet few managers get this. They miss out on the very best opportunity for developing their people – and at no extra cost.

They give them time off for training, but often in skills that don't quite fit. They assume that what's learned outside will be automatically turned into action inside. And they do little to groom people for the jobs of tomorrow through the work of today.

Yet simply by changing the way they involve their employees, and treat them, they could grow them more effectively than by any other means. At the same time, they would imbue in them the sense of purpose and meaning that, as I have mentioned, is the ultimate motivator.

Simply by changing their workplace conversations, by seeing themselves and their experienced colleagues as teachers and mentors – and every interaction as an opportunity for teaching and learning – and by investing time and effort in sharing their knowledge, they would see an improvement in both skills and motivation. And only by doing this will growth leadership become a reality.

There's plenty of advice on leadership. But here we are, after decades of T-groups, sensitivity training, servant leadership, emotional intelligence – and any number of other notions and nostrums regarding people and performance – with this simple and very obvious guide to creating a high-performance workplace:

1. Treat people fairly, respectfully, and consistently.
2. Give them important work, big challenges, clear goals, authority to make meaningful decisions, and responsibility for results.
3. Communicate openly and honestly with them, and shower them with more information than they need.
4. Listen to their suggestions, opinions, and concerns, and above all, to their feelings.
5. Provide the information, resources, and support that enable them to excel.
6. Involve them in "big conversations" and treat their inputs seriously.
7. Give them fast, honest, and helpful feedback on their performance.
8. Celebrate their wins and help them grow through failure.
9. Link rewards to performance, and show that there are consequences for non-performance or behaviours at odds with organizational expectations.
10. Think of the workplace as a classroom, and do whatever it takes to give people the richest possible learning opportunity in it.

Given how much money there is to make from breakthrough concepts, you can be sure that plenty of people will try to pull better rabbits out of the hat than these. But this formula has always applied – even if firms have been slow to apply it. And it will still be the one you need in 2020 … 2050 … and beyond.

Leadership is not a mysterious concept. It all comes down to the way you frame the space in which people work, and how you help them frame the world. It has always been this way, and always will be. And we know exactly how to do both things.

"Growth leadership" is not a catchphrase. Nor is it just for the few. It must be an everyday practice, and be evident everywhere. So it must be a core philosophy in your company which is embraced by everyone – but most especially by anyone with any responsibility for the performance of others.

PRACTICE #2:
Fast learning and adaptation

In our VUCA environment, the pace of change and its magnitude vary from industry to industry, but all firms have to deal with constant surprise and threats of disruption. All executives have to make decisions for a future they can't see.

They have to keep making those ten-buck bets. And the stakes are high.

No method exists to provide perfect foresight. No amount of scenario-planning, SWOT exercises, or big-data crunching will do it. Predictions are big business, but fortune-tellers and other futurists have an abysmal record.[8]

- Shell has used scenarios for more than 30 years, and is their most famous champion. But even so, the company missed three of the most significant changes of the early 21st century: China's sudden emergence as an economic power, the anti-globalization movement, and the spread of global terrorism.[9]
- Nate Silver has a formidable reputation as a statistician, and might have been remarkably accurate in forecasting the outcome of the 2008 and 2012 US presidential elections, but he can no more see the future than can anyone else.[10] His predictions for the 2015 UK general election were way off beam.[11] And like almost every other pollster, he failed to call Donald Trump's victory in the 2016 US presidential race.
- The "black swans" that Nassim Taleb warns about are everywhere. "Almost everything in social life is produced by rare but consequential shocks and jumps," he says, "almost everything

studied about social life focuses on the 'normal,' particularly with 'bell curve' methods of inference that tell you close to nothing."[12] Yet shortly after his book *The Black Swan* hit the shelves in April 2007, and then flew off to become a bestseller and make "black swans" an everyday term, the Great Crash caught all but a few economy watchers off guard. Then came the Arab Spring, the rise of ISIS, the collapse in the oil price, Russia's invasion of Crimea, and so on – with none of us any the wiser about what's next.

"We are blinder than we think," says the bestselling economics writer Tim Harford.[13] And that includes all of us.

But there's little pity for managers who blame their poor performance on unexpected shifts in the world around them. No matter what comes at them, they're expected to deliver. They have to produce results, even in the "fog of war."

There's obviously a role for systematic forecasting techniques. But while these might usefully inform decisions, they don't eliminate all risk or guarantee successful outcomes. There are two weaknesses in all of them.

First, they're based on *assumptions*, which may be based on facts but ultimately come down to opinion. And no matter how diligently you hone your assumptions, you will get some of them wrong.

Second, there comes a time when you have to make *choices* and lay your bets. No matter how many "what ifs" you consider, you have to pick one. So carefully developing a range of scenarios might alert you to various possibilities, and get you thinking about the best way to deal with each of them. Or backing your Plan A with a Plan B and Plan C – or even Plan X, Y, or Z – might offer comfort that you've considered all probabilities and options, and packed parachutes "just in case." But neither will ensure that you make the right call.

In fact, nothing will. Not even the advent of big data, or the unimaginable power of tomorrow's computers.

There will never be certainty in strategy. The number of variables that affect it will continue to proliferate. Pinning down patterns in them will become more scientific, but randomness and surprise will always lurk. Machines will facilitate and accelerate decision-making, but fallible humans will still have the last word.

The only practical way to keep your firm relevant – and *alive* – in an ever-changing context is to be hyper-alert to what's going on, and speedily adapt your strategy and operational activities to new circumstances. So as a matter of extreme urgency, you need to build adaptation into every fibre of your organization.

The starting point is to develop four specific capabilities that make riding the waves of change everybody's work:

1. *Sensing* change early and *making sense of it.*
2. *Imagining* possibilities.
3. *Doing* something about them.
4. *Reflecting* on what's happened in order to learn and exploit experience, build new strengths, and maybe adjust course.

These capabilities are linked in a continuous cycle. They frame what you and your colleagues need to talk about as you deal with the challenges of the day, so they're the golden thread of your strategic conversation and thus the essence of the strategy process (Figure 3.2). And since they're also a natural *outcome* of that conversation, the surest way to develop them is simply to keep referring to them and reminding people of their importance.

Figure 3.2

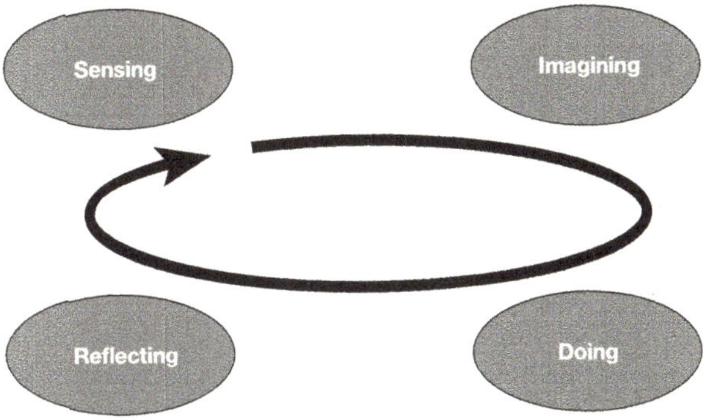

Because even insignificant human interactions are essential enablers of fast-cycle learning and adaptation, almost all of them provide opportunities to make your company more alert and more agile. There are three ways to make sure that they work for you:

1. Make a big thing about the four capabilities. Post a picture of the cycle on your walls. Encourage people to ask, before any speech, any meeting, any decision, or any change: Which of the four skills is this about? How can we make the most of it in what we're about to do?
2. Since you can't know who among your employees will offer the next insight or idea that could change your business, go with the wisdom of crowds. Make information widely available. Encourage people to read, watch the news, and debate current affairs. Open up lines of communication. Tell people you value their views, and encourage *all* of them to speak up. Ensure that they're heard – and that they know it. Ask probing questions. Ask for insights, ideas, and advice. Dish out praise at

every opportunity. And perhaps offer incentives for the really good stuff.

3. Assign small teams to concurrent activities and lots of low-cost experiments. Break down tasks so they can be shared among individuals and groups, with tight timelines for results. Make rapid feedback normal. And as the aim of this process is learning and adaptation, and not perfection, go out of your way to applaud both success and failure.

In the race to the future, "fast-cycle strategy" provides valuable advantages, so it has to be a way of life in every part of every organization.[14] Sensing, imagining, doing, and reflecting affect everything your company does and the way it does everything. So constant effort must be made to entrench and strengthen these capabilities – and to moving through these steps faster than your competitors.

You will no doubt have noticed that this cycle doesn't only explain the strategy process, but also *precisely maps the change-management process* (page 83). The very actions that ensure your company's survival, and are key to its growth, are the same as those that are essential in driving change – and thus in leadership, quality improvement, continuous improvement, and innovation:*

---

* Similar cycles underpin the advice of pioneers of the quality movement (remember the Plan-Do-Check-Adjust method advocated by Deming and Shewhart), and of the latest thinking in that field (Jeffrey K. Liker, *The Toyota Way*, New York: McGraw-Hill, 2004). They also form the basis of current military practice. And they've been implicitly or explicitly suggested by authorities on learning, leadership, and strategy, such as Chris Argyris (*Knowledge for Action*, San Francisco: Jossey-Bass, 1993); Noel Tichy (*The Cycle of Leadership*, New York: HarperBusiness, 2002); Karl E. Weick and Kathleen M. Sutcliffe (*Managing the Unexpected*, New

- **Sensing** change almost always triggers **dissatisfaction with the status quo.**
- **Imagining possibilities** is most likely when you **debate possible futures.**
- **Doing** things means **action,** and it's by acting that you **learn.**
- **Reflecting** is a vital aspect of **reviewing** progress, and of knowing what to **revise.**

By enlisting all your people as your firm's eyes and ears, and involving them deeply in important conversations whenever you can, you gain in multiple ways.

For one thing, they'll become aware that change is a crucial aspect of competitiveness – and that *they* have an important role in strategy.

Second, they'll alert you early to what's changing in and around your organization, and what might need attention, and they'll bring you suggestions for dealing with it.

Third, they'll be motivated to act when called on to do so.

And fourth – and here's a huge bonus – they'll learn about strategy and develop their own strategic IQ.

All this is free.

So simply by staying alert and deliberately talking about what's going on, conditions are created for change. And your firm becomes more fleet of foot and more agile.

York: John Wiley & Sons, 2007); Donald Sull (*The Upside of Turbulence*, New York: HarperCollins, 2009); Willie Pietersen (*Strategic Learning*, New York: John Wiley & Sons, 2010); Peter J. Williamson and Eden Yin ("Accelerated Innovation: The New Challenge from China," *Sloan Management Review*, Summer 2014); Eric Ries (*The Lean Startup*, New York: Crown Business, 2011); and Philip Tetlock and Dan Gardner (*Superforecasting*, New York: Random House, 2016).

These discussions should happen not just in strategy meetings, but in other meetings too. They should also happen at the water cooler or over a sandwich at lunch – in fact, almost any time people get together. This keeps the need for change top-of-mind, and makes your employees less inclined to resist it. And it not only triggers "what if" thinking, but also entrenches it in your company culture.

For conversations to have value, they must be about the *real issues* – both positive and negative – that affect organizations. And since we live in an unsettled world, and bad news is so prevalent, bad news is likely to get a lot of airtime.

This may raise fears, which can immobilize people. But it also presents an opportunity, as it can increase their dissatisfaction with the status quo, and spur them into action.

So here, as in defining your company's situation, you need to be sensitive to what's being said, and to the tone and the mood, and balance reality and hope in your strategic conversation.

PRACTICE #3:
Focus, value, costs

The critical core is a system. Every practice counts. But this one *defines strategy and is the reason for the others.*

There are more theories of competitive strategy than any executive needs. But when you get past their labels, and the sometimes extravagant claims made for them, they're mostly intended to solve this problem:

> *How to capture and keep the most attractive customers, and make acceptable and sustainable profits in the face of hostile competition.*

Military forces have faced a similar challenge over many centuries, although for them it's about seizing the most advantageous position in a conflict, controlling valuable territory, and ultimately gaining political power. Through hard-won experience, they made "concentration of forces" – i.e., of *resources* – the most basic principle of warfare. (Yet another example of the importance of the Ten-Buck Test!)

Business thinkers have always borrowed liberally from battlefield strategy, so the need to focus resources on opportunities has become a key tenet of corporate rivalry too. Except that in business we call it *positioning.*

The rationale is simple: to be a winner in a crowded world, you have to attract the attention of customers. They're busy and have many options. You don't have the resources to chase them all. So you have to pick your target carefully. And you have to *stand for something* that matters to those customers, and *stand out* from your competitors by being clearly different from them.

Positioning occurs in two ways: through your choices about *where to play* and *how to play*. The first involves your selection of which customers to focus on, with what features and benefits. The second has to do with how you want those customers to perceive you – what they should know and feel about your offering, and what they should experience in buying and using it.

Some markets are easier to penetrate and defend than others, and some may appear to be especially profitable. So according to one school of experts, led by Michael Porter, your choice of where to play is potentially a life-or-death issue.*

But it doesn't have to be, if you move beyond thinking about positioning as a once-off decision, and understand it instead as the *dynamic process* that it should be. And if you relentlessly pursue the "searing insights" that will bring the product and market opportunities your competitors don't see. Your choice of how to play is what ultimately matters, and there are many examples of firms that make healthy profits in "lousy" markets.

Positioning must be the first and most basic outcome you aim for in *crafting* your strategy. Whatever sector you compete in, and whatever you sell, you'll fare best if you focus your resources on the "right" customer for you, and avoid slipping into spray-and-pray mode in an attempt to satisfy everyone. You need to keep reminding your people of the need to do this, and test everything you do, and the way you do everything, against your positioning intention. Only by doing this can you cost-effectively establish and

---

* His popular five-forces framework helps firms find the most sustainably profitable market position for themselves (Michael E. Porter, *Competitive Strategy*, New York: The Free Press, 1980).

communicate your "difference" and why it matters, and put in place a way to deliver that difference.

Drucker's *who*, *what*, and *how* questions are evident here. They demand hard choices. But no matter how astute your initial answers may be, they alone won't keep your company competitive for long. To cling to the notion that you can plan a perfect strategy around them, and then sit back and watch the money roll in, is to ignore reality.

Just look around you. Watch competition unfolding in almost any sector today. You'll be astonished at how few firms are able to hold onto whatever space they wish to occupy in the market or in customers' minds. And this despite their best efforts to determine exactly where to aim.

Consider the logic of a typical approach to competitive strategy:

1. Different customers seek different value, which they assess by the performance and price of the products and services they buy. By and large, they all want to get as much as possible, and pay as little as possible. But they range along a spectrum, with those who want maximum performance at whatever price at one end, and those who'll be satisfied with much less – but at the lowest possible price – at the other.
2. By setting clear criteria for which of them to chase and who to ignore, you narrow your target market and improve your chances of success. You define your right customer – the customer who's best for you – by considering factors such as their profit potential, their expectations, how easy it will be to reach and attract them, your after-sales obligations to them, what they'll do for your reputation, what you'll learn from them, how they pay, what competitors offer them, and so on. You then

weigh up your choice of customer against your *real* ability to capture and keep them. And you're ruthless about scratching from your prospect list anyone who doesn't meet your criteria.

3. Once you know where you're going to focus, you ask: What is our difference, and why does it matter to that customer? And using your knowledge of them, and of your competitors, you create a compelling value proposition.
4. Finally, you think about what it'll take to deliver on your promise, and you design a business model to do it.

So far, so good. This, according to much of what's said about strategy, will give you a unique advantage. And even better – a *sustainable* advantage.

You could do all the necessary thinking on your own. Or perhaps with a small team. Or you could leave it to a strategy department or consulting firm, and simply endorse whatever they come up with. But even the smartest decisions provide no more than a *starting point* from which to pursue competitiveness. They'll get you only so far. And to make them with the inputs of only a few people is not the best way to go about it.

The overall context is in turmoil. Customers are a moving target, with changing needs, wants, and buying behaviours. Competitors innovate and improve relentlessly, make new promises, and drive down prices. Whatever value you offer today will doubtless have a short shelf life. Almost any advantage is *unsustainable.*

The only way to keep up, let alone get ahead and stay there, is to get inside your customers' heads, understand what turns them on, and stay attuned to how they're changing. And to *own their attention* by continuing to deliver the new performance and price they seek – or cannot yet imagine.

This means you have to do two seemingly contradictory things at the same time:

1. **Cultivate the deepest possible sense of how customers see their situation and their challenge,[*] and relentlessly *drive their perceptions of value up.***
2. **Apply the Ten-Buck Test to everything you do and the way you do everything, and relentlessly push for efficiencies and savings to *drive costs down.*[†]**

As always, these involve information, analysis, and hard choices – the traditional stuff of strategy. They also require the design and development of an appropriate way to deliver value, and skill in execution.

But there's a greater challenge. And it's not one you can overcome permanently through surveys or desk work, or in a few meetings or workshops. Or through richer data or smarter forecasting techniques, or even by reengineering your processes or structure. It is, of course, the *social* aspect of organizational life – which affects everything you do and the way you do everything.

To continually adapt and flex your business model, and race along the twin paths of value-up, costs-down, calls for the imagin-

---

* This is the basis for your value proposition – just as clarity about your *firm's* situation and challenge is the basis of your overall strategy. Even if you initially turn a blind eye to customers' views, and offer them products or services for which there's no apparent need, what you can learn from them can make you a winner in the long run.

† Note that we're talking here about *costs*, not prices. Only by driving costs down can you sustain margins while either cutting prices or investing in new value; it also gives you the option of holding your prices and capturing extra margin. And it's necessary even if you *raise* your prices, because without this discipline, costs can quickly spin out of control.

ation, initiative, enthusiasm, energy, collaboration, and hard work of people across your firm – and of other business partners too. No amount of thought or planning will unleash these, and you can't impose them. Nor will capital investment or technology or systems do it on their own.

Quite simply, key stakeholders must *volunteer* themselves to this task, or you'll never do as well as you want to.

Getting the results you want begins with your embracing the fact that *strategy is a living process, and competitiveness is a moving target.*

Both rely on rapid improvement and innovation, flexibility, and adaptation. These have to be integral aspects of your work life, and not ideals that you pursue one at a time alongside "real" work, or as projects that you slot into your "real" work.

Motivation and attitude obviously play a central role in ensuring you get this right. But while they're invaluable catalysts, they're by no means all it takes. So even while you talk up your team, you have to deal with *all* the elements that will make your strategy effective.

All the other critical strategy practices must kick in and support your focus-value-cost intention (Figure 3.3).

As this model shows, there are many criteria by which to define your right customer and thus concentrate your forces. There are also many ways to create a "difference that matters" to those customers. And when you couple these insights to the countless others in the rest of the critical core, you'll surely find more than enough opportunities to improve your competitiveness.

Military practice continues to stress the need for "concentration of forces," but fixed battles involving masses of troops and

Figure 3.3

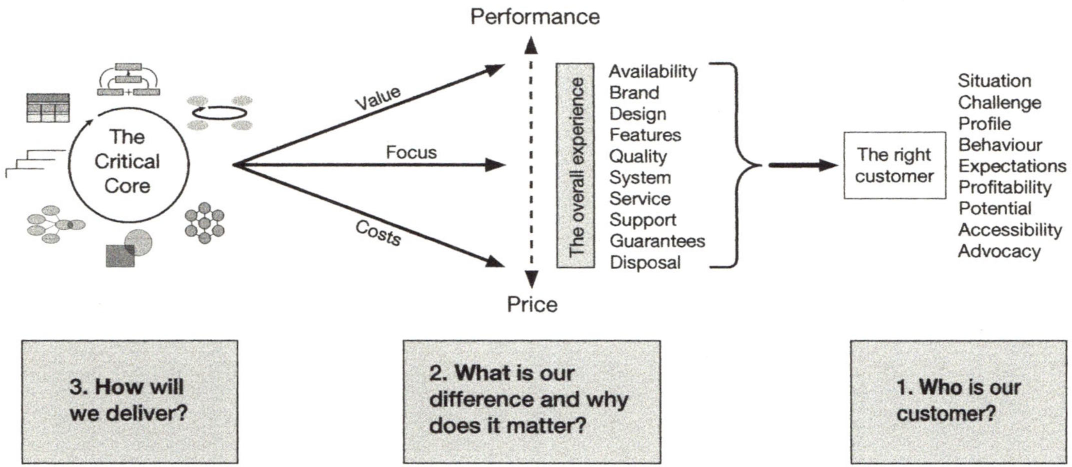

Performance
Price
The Critical Core
Value
Focus
Costs
The overall experience
Availability
Brand
Design
Features
Quality
System
Service
Support
Guarantees
Disposal
The right customer
Situation
Challenge
Profile
Behaviour
Expectations
Profitability
Potential
Accessibility
Advocacy
3. How will we deliver?
2. What is our difference and why does it matter?
1. Who is our customer?

weaponry are being supplanted by hit-and-run sorties by small teams. They're informed by rigorous intelligence gathering, and equipped and trained to move fast and change tactics with the flow of combat. And through after-action reviews, they make every engagement a source of learning for the next one.

Surprisingly, though, business has been slow to adopt the lessons of its revered teachers.

Crafting a strategic conversation sets the scene for the outcomes you want. But only by *conducting* that conversation with skill and sensitivity to your context, so that necessary decisions and actions follow, will you actually achieve those outcomes – or better.

Focus, value, and costs – and not just focus – must be constant themes in your strategic conversation, or your business will not be around for long. It always has been that way, and it always will be. All that's changed is the speed at which you have to advance.

Much as you may wish for a different answer to the competitiveness challenge, there isn't one. *There is no other way to compete and win.* Another clever matrix won't do it for you. Nor will Porter's five forces, a balanced scorecard, or Clayton Christensen's theory of disruption. Or any other strategy tool.

Of course, business thinkers will keep churning out "new" concepts of strategy. But whatever they concoct will inevitably be based on this framework. There will be novel twists, no doubt, but the basics will remain the same.

You will always have to answer the who, what, how questions. You'll always have to "concentrate your forces." And you'll never escape the need to combine firm decisions with flexible behaviour.

Focus will always matter, and driving value up and costs down will become increasingly important. So the insights I've offered about change management, strategic IQ, leadership, disciplined execution, and fast-cycle learning and adaptation will become increasingly relevant.

And the reluctance of many of your competitors to accept and apply these, or their hesitation in doing so, will make it easier than you think to get the edge over them.

PRACTICE #4:
Business model innovation

A company is a value-delivery machine. Its business model is its idea of how it creates, delivers, and captures value for its various stakeholders – which frames key choices, and depicts them as a system. Whether explicit or implicit, every company has such a concept – or "blueprint."

Because business conditions change constantly, and companies must keep offering new value, business models can become obsolete while you're thinking about other things. What works in one period is likely to be a recipe for failure in another. The race to the future is essentially a race for business model innovation.

Ideally, your theory of success should guide the design of your business model. But what actually happens is often different.

A firm's concept of how it should function typically takes shape over time, and not altogether deliberately, as it works out how to survive. Changes occur here and there within the organization. Interest in yesterday's practices wanes. New practices creep in, some of them unseen. The theory of success – if ever it existed – morphs into something else.

The founders of upstart, internet-centric firms make a great thing about their business models, but others mostly don't. They fret over specifics such as strategy, their product offerings, and their organizational structure or processes, but fail to address their value system in a holistic way by asking: How can we reframe our business to produce different results?

This makes them vulnerable in the short term, and doubtless hurts their profits in the long term. It also lessens their chances of finding better ways to compete in a different future. And every commitment they make to their *current* model – those ten-buck investments – makes inertia more likely for reasons I've spelled out.

One excuse for not thinking about your business model is that "What we're doing works." Another is that other matters seem more urgent. But the most common reason is that managers simply lack a way to address the issue.

Although the term "business model" is bandied about by analysts and business journalists, it appears far less often in business books or serious journals, or is buried amid other matters. It's hardly ever highlighted as being critical, and it doesn't feature prominently in business agendas.

In fact, there's nothing mysterious about business model design. As my "7Ps" framework shows (Figure 3.4), it involves a set of key factors which add up to a view of where and how you compete.

Figure 3.4

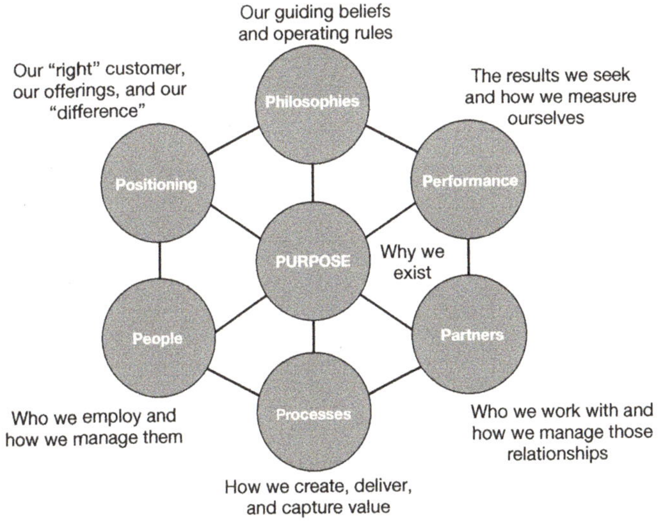

Thinking through them separately and in combination will help you evaluate your present competitive strength, identify your weaknesses, and hopefully see new possibilities.

It should also foster conversation about the *linkages* between the elements. For like a system of gears, the components obviously have to fit snugly together and turn smoothly. So they must be carefully chosen, they must all mesh with each other, and the effect of each must be amplified through skilful execution. The whole must be greater than the sum of the parts.

I developed this framework after London Business School professor Sumantra Ghoshal and Christopher Bartlett, a professor at Harvard Business School, published a series of three articles in *Harvard Business Review* in 1994–95, based on a five-year study of 20 successful global firms.*

"Senior managers of today's large enterprises must move beyond strategy, structure, and systems," they argued, "to a framework built on purpose, process, and people." This was necessary because "the great power – and fatal flaw – of the strategy-structure-systems framework lay in its objective: to create a management system that could minimize the idiosyncrasies of human behavior."[15]

That was a light-bulb moment for me. I had always been convinced that the role of people in strategy was underplayed, and I'd been thinking for a long time about how to elevate it. The 7S framework developed by McKinsey and made famous by Tom Peters and Bob Waterman in *In Search of Excellence* went some way towards this, but fell short as an aid to designing business models. I'd published an article of my own just before the Ghoshal–Bartlett

---

* Their findings were later published in their excellent book, *The Individualized Corporation* (New York: HarperBusiness, 1997).

series, in which I outlined a model for strategic thinking comprising seven elements; I called it the 7Ps.[16]

But now I immediately saw the potential for creating an improved framework, specifically as an aid to business model design. One that would not only take into account those troublesome "idiosyncrasies of human behaviour," but also help ensure that they stayed front and centre in managers' thinking. And after interviewing Bartlett by phone,[17] I added four more elements than he and Ghoshal had highlighted, and created a new framework – again called the 7Ps.* Every part of it either affects people or is affected by them.

When you design your business model – or redesign it – think about this:

Purpose – Every business leader must ask and answer two of Drucker's favourite questions: "What is the business?" and "What should it become?" He was probably the first to describe these as its mission and vision. But as I pointed out in Chapter 2, these terms are so badly misused and abused that there's a strong case for favouring purpose. Chances are you'll be able to say it in fewer words – and more clearly – than if you go the mission-vision route.

A compelling purpose obviously helps you align efforts, coordinate activities, and apply resources in an integrated way. It thus informs each of the other six elements of the framework, and ensures that they work as a whole.

But more than that, it frees you from the urge to use strategy to prescribe every move far into the future.

---

* The version here is yet a further update, with Products having been replaced by Performance. It's the result of more than 20 years of trial and error, with numerous clients.

Telling your team, "We're going for Hill X, not Hill Y or Z," is a first step towards empowering people to contribute their own ideas about how to get there. And it's essential if they're to be trusted to make appropriate decisions in the heat of battle, perhaps far from home, without having to keep referring back to a strategy document or a boss.

Philosophies – These are the guiding beliefs and "operating rules" that affect every area of a business, from its Purpose to its market Positioning, from its Performance criteria to its People, and from the way it engages with the Partners in its ecosystem to its Processes (the other six Ps).

Examples of questions to ask: Should we go for top-end customers, or chase those for whom price is everything? Should we make or buy what we sell? Should we encourage open innovation or pursue new ideas in-house? What kinds of people should we hire and what should be our approach to managing them? How will we balance our responsibilities to various stakeholders? How should we handle difficult customers, or complaints and service issues? Should we be diligent about maintenance, or fix things only when there's an accident or a breakdown? How far should we go in caring for the environment? How should we deal with corporate governance and ethical dilemmas?

One firm's philosophy will be to invest in bleeding-edge technologies; another will invest more cautiously. One will have a hearty risk appetite, while another will be happier with smaller bets. One will try to keep a mature business alive at all costs, while another will deliberately kill yesterday's cash cows and constantly seek new growth opportunities.

By *proactively* thinking through the assumptions that underpin your theory of success, you avoid having to do so when you're under pressure or somehow caught off guard. You also ensure that your Ps are aligned, and that people won't make on-the-hoof decisions about one of them that clash with those about the rest.

Together with your purpose, your philosophies are a means to empowerment. When you make them clear, everyone knows what matters to the organization, what's expected of them, and what's acceptable or not. And you go some way towards helping them with the difficult dilemmas and trade-offs they'll encounter in their daily work.

Most firms today have a values statement, and yours may indeed deal with some of the issues mentioned here. But it's not enough to trot out words like "integrity," "ethical," "responsibility," and "excellence." Everyone says these things, and they may well be very important to you. But you need to go much further, so I'm talking about something different and more comprehensive.

This doesn't imply yet another long list of fine intentions. What it does mean is that you should give a lot of thought and much discussion to your overall *point of view about doing business.*

Positioning – This is where you decide: Who is our "right" customer? What is our "difference" (the value you offer) and why does it matter?

To make wise choices, you need as rich an understanding as possible of your customers and your competitors, of the dynamics at play in the marketplace, and of the trends or forces that might disrupt them.

It's one thing to choose a position, and quite another to defend it against aggressive competitors. Is this *possible*? For how long? What will you have to do to hold onto it? What will cause its value to erode? Who might threaten you, and how? What might cause your customers to change their relationships with you, or leave?

Positioning can be a powerful source of competitive advantage, and should be top of mind in every strategic conversation. But in most industries, it's becoming less easy to sustain whatever advantages it confers. So *continually learning from customers, developing new offerings, and executing with excellence* are accordingly becoming more critical.

Unexplored markets are few and far between, and once-attractive niches are being carved up. More analysis and slicing-and-dicing will bring diminishing returns. Nor are branding and customer loyalty programmes any assurance of future sales or profits.

You may out*think* your rivals for a while, and should strive to do this; but you should also aim to out*run* them, by doing what you do better and faster than they can. It's the only way to win over the long haul.

Performance – To be competitive, companies must excel in a range of activities. So they have to set goals and measure their internal and external performance using a variety of metrics. They must know how their people are doing, how costs and sales are trending, how productive their factories and call centres are, how customers rate them, how they compare to their rivals, and much else.

But in their efforts to be thorough, and to control as much as they can, most of them strive to be too precise about too much, and put numbers to things that can't be measured or that they needn't bother with. So scorecards, dashboards, and spreadsheets clutter desks, walls, and presentations, and have become dumping grounds for every imaginable scrap of information about what must be done, what has been done, and how well it was done.

In fact, *there's no need to know everything about everything.* A simple set of metrics will serve most firms – and certainly most of their people – perfectly well. So you need to decide what matters to you, what you *have* to know, and how the information will be accessed, presented, or used. And you need to fight the temptation to add more and more, by constantly reminding yourself of the risks of overload and complexity.

With growth leadership as your aim, it makes sense to test every metric by a single question: *Will it help us grow the business, and do it by growing the people?*

The answer will mostly be no.

On the other hand, a few key measures ensure that you home in on what you must change, and keep a constructive conversation flowing between you and your people. And that's as good as it gets.

People – This covers everything from who you hire to your company climate, culture, and management approach; and from your organization's structure and HR arrangements to training and development. This is where growth leadership comes into play.

Customers aside, there's no aspect of business where good intentions are less evident than in these matters. In almost every strategy assignment I've ever worked on, people have featured surprisingly low on the agenda. Assertions about people being "our most important asset," or ambitions to be "a great place to work," are mostly hollow. Yet, without people, an organization is nothing. No other factor has the same impact on results.

Every firm needs people with the right mix of skills, attitudes, and experience. Some know exactly who they've got and where the gaps are, and have excellent recruitment and development programmes. But many are uncertain about who's there and who they need – or who they should let go. They're slack about replenishing their pipeline, their retention efforts are misguided, and development is an afterthought.

Very few decisions about people can be made on a purely rational basis. Here, perhaps more than in any of the other elements of your business model, your core beliefs – your philosophies – can and should override all else. So you need to be especially aware of them, and take them into account in your decisions. If you ignore them, you might strike it lucky with some of your choices, but it's far likelier you'll make lots of costly mistakes.

Partners – Even small firms today have more stakeholders than in the past. A swarm of players influence their ability to function and their competitiveness (see Critical Practice #6), so building sound relationships with them has to be high on any strategist's agenda. This is especially the case with those stakeholders you describe as business partners.

Investors, suppliers, your people, and their labour unions naturally fall into this category. But you need to look outside of your organization too.

Work is increasingly outsourced or given to temporary workers. Supply chains are becoming more complex, and suppliers and distributors play a growing role in value-adding processes. So do *customers*, who are becoming "prosumers." And research scientists, financiers, and advertising agencies all contribute directly to your success.

You might have established relationships with many of these today. But are you getting all you need from them? Are there other ways you might collaborate with them? Are there more you should be working with?

Processes – The results you get in your business are a product of *what you do* to create, deliver, and capture value. As growing competition makes it harder to "make a difference that matters" to your customers, what happens inside your business becomes increasingly important. Only by choosing different processes than your competitors, or performing them differently or better, can you hope to succeed.

Every function, from R&D and administration to manufacturing and marketing, involves multiple processes. So there's a selling process, an order-fulfilment process, a production process, and so on. Each of these involves a specific set of *activities*, which in turn involve various *actions*. Some of these are routine, and can be solidly embedded into your company. Others only come into play from time to time, so there has to be a way to initiate them – often very quickly – when you need them, and to let them go when they've done their thing.

Many processes are internal, and under your control. But many occur externally, and coordination and control can be extremely testing. Your skills here are a key source of strength or weakness.

Processes are just one element of your business model, and most are elements in a *system of processes*. So they have to not only fit and enhance your overall business model, but also fit together and enhance each other. Only when they do both will you be able to drive value up and costs down. If they don't, you'll destroy value and add costs.

Before you settle on any process, be clear about what you expect it to do. Ask: Is this the best way to achieve the results we want? How will it affect whatever else we do? Will it enable us to scale up our business? And look ahead and consider how you might make it more valuable in the future, and when and how you might need to improve or replace it, or do something else altogether. What will your options be then? What will *their* impact be? What else will you have to change?

Remember, from the moment you adopt a new process, and especially when it comes with big costs and a need for learning, path dependence kicks in. So you need to be as sure as possible that what you begin will take you where you intend going, and that you'll be able to make it more of a strength over time, rather than being thwarted by it.

The 7Ps framework is a diagnostic tool that encompasses both the hard and the soft issues that contribute to your competitiveness. It helps you systematically unpack your organization, poke into its innards, and engage your team in new conversations. This obviously should be done with some regularity – perhaps as part of your normal planning process. But it will have even greater value to you if you reflect on it continuously.

Every aspect of your business model is in constant flux. Every one of the 7Ps offers opportunities to make your firm more competitive. Only by thinking about them one at a time, *all the time* – and *all together* as well – will you exhaust all your possibilities.

Until then, don't assume you've run out of ways to improve your performance. Until you've taken your business model apart and thought about each element of it, and considered how they interact with each other, you're probably forgoing opportunities for profit and growth.

PRACTICE #5:
Resource and capability acquisition, development, and leverage

A company's resources (the inputs it requires to create value) and capabilities (the skills and processes that enable it to turn those resources into value) are vital assets (Figure 3.5). Competitiveness originates in the way they're combined and exploited, and they define the game a company can play and how it can play.[18*] And since their value erodes as circumstances change, they need to be constantly added to, enhanced, or replaced.

Figure 3.5

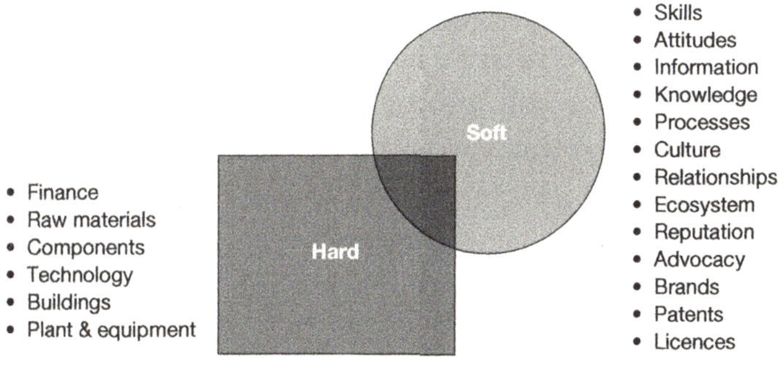

Some resources are "hard" – they're "things" or "stuff," so they're generally visible. Others are "soft" – they're knowledge-based.

---

* The resource-based view of the firm (RBV), core competence, and dynamic capabilities all rest on such combinations and mean essentially the same thing: *what enables you to compete.*

Some are rare, costly, and hard to get or develop, maintain, and keep. Others may be quickly, readily, and even cheaply available; they're there for anyone who wants them and will pay for them. So for many firms they're no longer the competitive advantage they once were – *unless they are used in new ways.*

Capabilities are a different matter altogether. They enable you to use resources effectively, and find new ways to apply them. They're always soft, so you can't buy them off the shelf. What's more, it almost always takes time for them to show their true value.

For example:

- It can take years to build a brand or a reputation, or learn how to miniaturize an electronics product, build a "green" car, or operate in a foreign market.
- Mergers and acquisitions usually take much longer to bed down than anyone foresees, and the results are often disappointing, because of the difficulty in marrying capabilities and cultures.
- Even if you hire skilled people, it can take weeks for them to fit into your organization and many months for their knowledge to diffuse through your team.
- Packaged training programmes only show their value when what they teach becomes a way of life – which doesn't happen overnight.

When you assess the worth of resources and capabilities, beware of seeing value that's not there. Merely performing some or other activity doesn't make it a core competence or distinctive capability.

If customers don't care about what your combination of resources and capabilities does for them, they won't buy from you. If those resources and capabilities don't enable you to do something special for them, they won't pay your price. And if your resources and capabilities don't enable you to earn superior profits, there's not much point in them.[19]

Owning a fleet of trucks is of little benefit if competitors keep their costs lower than yours through leasing. Massive server farms and sexy algorithms won't give you an edge for long if others are able to copy you. Mastering the use of laser technology in your factory won't help you if the products you make don't offer customers unique and meaningful benefits.

On its own, an inside-out approach to strategy will never get you to the best combination of resources and capabilities. You have to take an outside-in view too, and shift back and forth between the two. And you have to keep revisiting your conclusions, adjusting your bundle of assets, and thinking of new ways to apply them.

Without a reasonably clear view of where you intend taking your company, your approach to developing resources and capabilities will be haphazard. You'll face constant dilemmas over where to spend your ten bucks. Instead of methodically and holistically bolstering your strengths, you'll waste money and effort on a stab here and a stab there. Nothing will ever gel as it should.

Paradoxically, since path dependence is an inevitable consequence of developing resources and capabilities, the very strengths that you need and that you develop in your business can lock it into a strategy that becomes inappropriate.[20] Changing direction may become extremely difficult and time-consuming – even impossible. So all commitments should be made with the agility of your organization top of mind. And you should continually consider ways to enhance that agility, such as outsourcing work, employing temps, leasing equipment on short-term contracts, or entering into partnerships with easy exit terms.[21]

Resources and capabilities are essential in your current business. But they also provide the basis of tomorrow's business. Leveraging them smartly and deliberately can give you a running start towards future opportunities.

As with most other aspects of strategy, the time to think about this is not *after* your strategy is done and dusted, or when you make your initial commitments. Path dependence will kick in faster than you imagine, so you'll gain most by taking a long view of your resources and capabilities, and their potential, as early as possible.

By continually considering, "*What else* we can do with them?" you'll almost certainly highlight new possibilities – and thus inspire new thinking about where you're going, and why, and how.

By continually asking, "*How else* can we use them?" you'll undoubtedly find ways to get more bang from your ten bucks.

And with every step you take into the future, your organization will grow stronger.

PRACTICE #6: Stakeholder alignment and support

Most companies today have an increasingly broad array of stakeholders who have some or other interest in them, and can effectively "vote" for or against their success. These might be individuals, groups, or organizations. Some will be more aligned with your goals than others. Their power varies too, and they exercise it in different ways.

Some, such as shareholders, staff, suppliers, distributors, and customers, are keen for you to succeed, are very directly involved with your business, and require constant attention. Others are less "in-your-face," less influential, and less demanding.

Competitors mostly want to make life hard for you, or are intent on seeing you fail.* Regulators can allow you to have a shot at success or *ensure* that you fail.

The media, lobbyists, and other activists hold powerful sway over your reputation and your ability to conduct your business (Figure 3.6).

The shape of this ecosystem and the power dynamics within it are sure to change as players come and go and change their minds.

As far as possible, these players must be persuaded to act in support of your firm's goals. To help rather than hinder you. To line up in total support of your efforts to build win-win relationships with customers (Figure 3.7).

---

* In some instances, "good competition" is in everyone's interests. The existence of a number of competitors may keep regulators off their backs, and some level of industry stability is good for profits. Competitors may also play other valuable roles – for example, as suppliers or distributors.

Figure 3.6

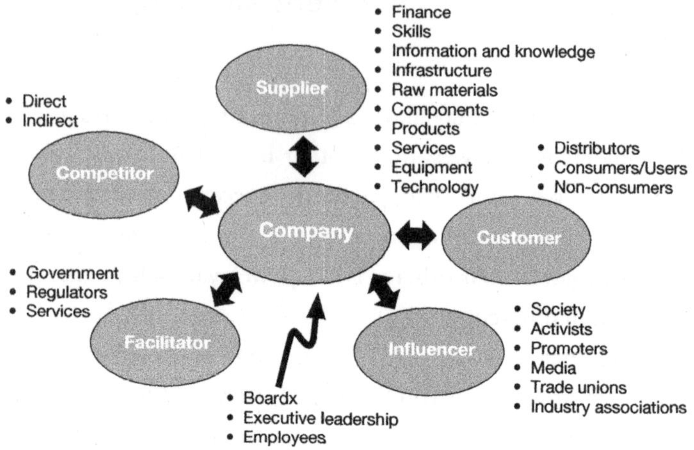

Stakeholder management is a never-ending communications challenge. It's one more reason for your strategy to be clear, and for all your people to understand your intentions.

To deal with this matter, you need to know who your stakeholders are, and how they influence your business. You need to understand their agendas, and what they can do to affect your fate. And you need to develop deliberate strategies for managing your relationships with them, and assign specific people to some of them, at least.*

Because all firms have many stakeholders, and interact with them in many ways – face to face; through various media; and via

---

* The need for stakeholder management applies similarly to "value ecosystems," open innovation, and crowdsourcing, all of which are being increasingly adopted as ways to accelerate innovation, cut costs, and lock in customers.

Figure 3.7

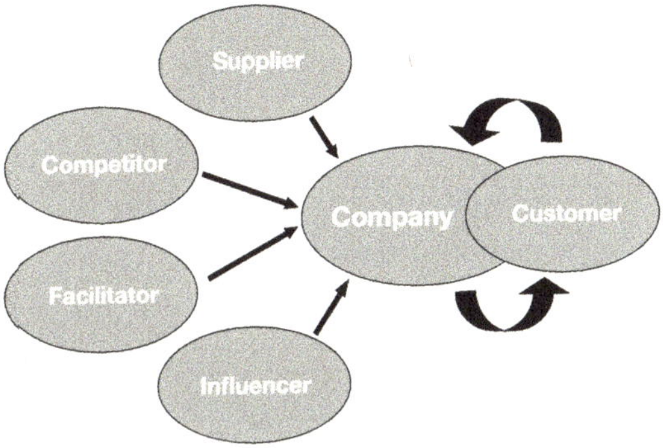

intermediaries, contracts, employee relations, logistical arrangements, services, structures, and an almost infinite number of others – this is not "a job" that can be left to a communications department.

It has to be firmly on the CEO's agenda.

And it has to be everybody's business.

And all the more so given the extreme risks firms face in this age of social media, when a single, seemingly innocuous comment by an employee can explode in a nanosecond. Or when almost anyone, anywhere, can set off a frenzy of criticism, and force a company into desperate damage-control mode.

PRACTICE #7:
Smart sequencing and pacing

Strategic planning is a taken-for-granted activity in most firms, albeit one with a dodgy reputation. It consistently ranks high among management tools, despite mounting evidence of its shortcomings. If ever there was an example of hope upstaging common sense, this is it.

In theory, plans – whether strategic, tactical, or operational – should be detailed and precise. In the real world, however, this often proves to be pointless. Any plan is only as sound as the assumptions it's based on, and these often turn out to be hopelessly flawed. The environment keeps changing in surprising ways, and what makes perfect sense one day makes none the next.

Meanwhile, new issues suddenly become priorities, critical projects hit potholes and delays, and costs run wild. Enthusiasm fizzles and, day by day, wonderful plans unravel and become increasingly irrelevant.

But this doesn't mean you don't need plans, or that you should give up on planning. What it does underscore is the necessity to be realistic about what's feasible and what you should aim to achieve. That while you need to be as specific as you can, you also need to allow yourself the space to change your mind. And that *crafting and conducting your strategic conversation is always a work in progress.*

To achieve what you intend for your company requires a roadmap of sorts, and some idea of how you'll get where you want to go. Resources are limited, and you can't do everything – and certainly not all at once. And as you advance, you have to coordinate a multiplicity of actions. So although you'll have to make many decisions on the fly, the process can't be altogether haphazard, nor can you leave everything to the winds of chance or the whims of the moment.

Countless issues scream for immediate attention, and you have to respond fast to many of them. But do they all affect the fundamental thrusts of your strategy, or make its key themes redundant? Definitely not. However, if there's a hint that any of them might, you need to pause for breath, get them into perspective, and carefully assess their implications.

A single issue can throw a strategy out of whack. But strategy is about more than one unanticipated problem or opportunity. Having done your thinking and made your choices, there are some things that you have to keep doing, in spite of noise around them.

Your larger decisions should be made, and acted on, in the order and at the time and speed that make most sense. Some must come before others, because they're building blocks for what follows and without a solid foundation you'll run into trouble later. Some must be swift, in order to seize an opportunity or steal a march on competitors – or just because it's possible. Always, you should try to move at the speed that suits you, rather than what's *apparently* dictated by some external force. And you need to be resolute about this, because more often than not you'll have more time than you're led to believe. Someone else's "urgent" doesn't have to be yours.

Being first to market can be an advantage. Getting in early lets you establish a base, grab the choicest customers, sign up the most powerful business partners, and possibly define the rules of the game. It also gives you time to learn how things actually work and to fine-tune your strategy.

On occasion, though, it'll be wiser to advance in a more measured way – to "sniff the wind," learn from the experience of others, and make your moves when you have a clearer sense of what it'll take to play and win.[22]

Penetrating any new market can take far longer and be far more difficult than you imagine. It's the same with launching a new product into an *existing* market, or changing some aspect of your strategy. There's always something to learn, and you have to put resources and capabilities in place. You might think you can move faster by skipping a few steps, but that might be impossible – or you might pay for it later. Moving too fast can be every bit as perilous as moving too slowly.

Stretch goals are a powerful way to unleash energy in a firm, but they need to be carefully balanced with "baby steps." Asking people to achieve things that are clearly out of the question is pointless and dispiriting. At best, they might get marginally further than they otherwise would have, but there's a risk that visions of achievement will be dampened by the reality of failure.

Project managers know that the best way to complete an assignment is to break it down into pieces, with tight but reasonable delivery dates for each of them, and to tackle first things first. They understand that success in one task motivates performance in the next. Yet, other executives tend to be cavalier about these matters, and often rush headlong into trouble as a result.

A useful way to map your path to the future is to draw what McKinsey refers to as a "strategy staircase" (later termed "horizons to growth"), which shows what you'll do in Year 1, Year 2, and so on (Figure 3.8).[23] Seen like this, it's apparent that some things simply cannot be done before others, no matter how keen you might be; that you have to learn to walk before you can run; and that all commitments have *consequences*.

Only with a sense of the big picture, and a reasonably long view, will you be likely to do more or less the right things, at the right times, and to put tomorrow's resources and capabilities in place where and when you need them. But even then, you shouldn't assume your firm will advance exactly as you intend. No company gets to the future in a straight line. Nor do many get where they want to go on time.

Things *will* go wrong. Your best-laid plans will crumble or blow up in your face. So you have to keep rethinking and adjusting your course and your activities, and the sequence and speed of your actions.

Figure 3.8

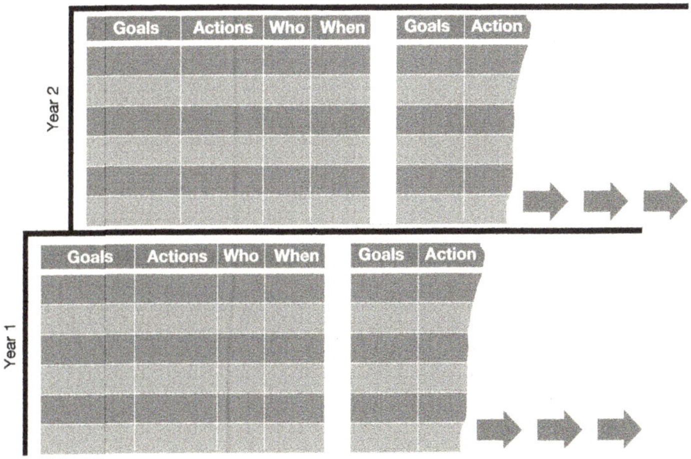

PRACTICE #8:
Disciplined execution

Planning a way forward is one thing. Making it happen is another challenge entirely. Designing strategy is invariably much easier than turning it into action. In fact, there's abundant evidence that poor execution, rather than deficient strategy, is the biggest impediment to growth in companies worldwide, and that corporate leaders see operational excellence as their number-one challenge.[24]

There are many reasons for this. But the root cause lies in our common perception of how to fix the problem. The usual formula goes like this:

1. Communicate the strategy to everyone who'll be involved in any way.
2. Make their goals and roles clear, and give them the resources and support they need.
3. Track their progress.
4. Hold them accountable for results, and reward them appropriately.

This sounds logical and straightforward, and looks like a helpful outline. But it assumes that execution is a mechanical process that comes *after* strategy, and is largely about telling people what they must do, checking how they fare, and keeping them on course.

It makes things sound much simpler than they are by also assuming that the announced strategy is as good as it gets, and there will be no surprises. That there's no need to involve people in making their own decisions, or for you to continually embrace new insights and encourage fresh thinking. And that if a strategy is explained it's understood, that people will spontaneously align themselves behind it, and that cooperation across functions will occur as a matter of course.

But mostly, this is not so.

The nifty little checklist ignores two costly disconnects between strategic intentions and results, so it reinforces a mistaken view of what execution really entails, and ensures that firms will keep getting it wrong.

Disconnect #1: Messages are lost in translation between the C-suite and the front line. Mixed messages are a fact of organizational life. It's normal for high-level strategy to be ignored, misinterpreted, or sidestepped at other levels – sometimes deliberately, but more often because nothing is clear. And managers themselves either cause or worsen both problems.

They overestimate their ability to make themselves understood, and underestimate how much ongoing time and effort it takes. They assume that saying something once is enough. And that what they say arrives in other people's heads exactly the way they said it, and means exactly what they intended. And they kid themselves that when they speak they're believed, and that people will do as they're told.

But the people who are supposed to turn decisions into action have minds of their own. They might not be paying attention, or they may simply choose to do something else. Or they might follow instructions, but execute them poorly. Or they fail to adapt as circumstances change.

Communication is without question the biggest challenge in any company. Most managers are lousy communicators. Just because we all do it every day is no reason to think it's easy or that we're good at it. More than anything else, it makes the difference between success and failure.

Disconnect #2: The future is highly unlikely to turn out as the masterminds upstairs assume it will. Despite their best efforts to stay in tune and in touch, they only become aware of many changes long after they've occurred – and certainly long after people anywhere near the action are able to sense them. By the time they snap into action, and get around to rethinking their strategy and issuing new orders, it's too late. And if, like so many, they adhere to a one-, three-, or five-year planning cycle, there's no chance that they can stay in sync with their context. A divide between what they *should do* and what they *in fact do* is assured. And the gap keeps getting wider.

These disconnects are so normal and so evident, and their impact so serious, that you'd think there would be more alarm about them. But managers keep getting predictable surprises on both counts. Things seldom work out as they expect. Their scintillating schemes are constantly upset by the unpredictability of the outside world, the internal machinations of their organizations, and human nature. Fine intentions turn out to be no match for harsh reality.

Forces are at work in almost every organization that can tear it apart and derail its strategy, and the purpose of management is to hold things together and enable firms to produce desirable results predictably and consistently. But they will only achieve the *best* results if they are able to balance control and conformity with freedom to dissent and experiment.

To do this, they need to understand execution in two ways.

First, it is *project management.*[25] Getting the results you want is too important to be left to chance or the whim of individuals. Some people may naturally get things done, so whenever possible they should be assigned to the most important activities. But no firm can rely on only the rare few with this ability. Nor can commitment or teamwork be taken for granted.

In the absence of discipline, things quickly go awry. Once a sense is created that there's no roadmap or any urgency about key actions, that ignoring pledges and missing deadlines is OK, and that excuses will be tolerated, the scene is set for trouble. A pervasive rot quickly sets in. The climate turns toxic. Complacency takes over, and the resulting lack of progress leads to further slackness. In no time, non-delivery becomes a habit and an underlying cultural assumption: "This is the way we do things around here."

So there needs to be a systematic way to get things done, and everyone must understand it and stick to it.

The challenge, however, is not just to get X or Y done, but how to get Eric or Jane – human beings with their own agendas, values, inclinations, and abilities – to do it. And to do it within a context of politics, pressure, resource constraints, constant interruptions, missteps, conflicts, and glitches.

The challenge, also, is to get Eric and Jane to go above and beyond the call of duty, and contribute even more than the strategy requires of them. And to ensure that when things change around them, they'll respond with insights and ideas that the ivory-tower planners might not be able to offer.

And this brings us to the second aspect of execution: the fact that *it's fundamentally a social process.*

Because it inevitably requires some kind of change, it depends every bit as much on the emotions and attitudes of individuals as on organizational structures, systems, or rules.

People need to understand a firm's purpose, its situation, and the challenge it faces. They need to know what its goals are and how these might be achieved, and who should do what by when to produce them. And, most crucially, they need to know how they personally fit into the picture.

But merely *telling* them all this – no matter how well you do it – won't suffice. One-way communication won't do it. You cannot ever safely assume that what you say is what people hear and understand, or that what you ask them to do is what they will do. Nor can you assume that people will give of their best when you haven't shaped the conditions in which it will happen. And this is where, yet again, your firm's strategic conversation and climate come into play.

I've said this before, but I'll say it again because it's so important:

Strategy is a process and not an event. It's dynamic and complex and reliant on people. So the only sensible time to start thinking about how to execute it is *when you begin crafting your strategic conversation.*

That's when you need to motivate people to let go of the past and accept the need for change, and when you need to ready them to do different things, and do things differently.

That's also when you need to make decisions about the activities and actions that will bring the results you want, along with ongoing improvement and innovation.

And it's when you start *conducting* the conversation that will take you in a new direction.

A vital yet underestimated arena for that conversation is the meetings in which you review progress. These can be viewed as a nuisance that takes you and your people away from "real" work, or as an opportunity for learning and growth. To waste them is a crime against your company – but that's exactly what many managers do.

Their reviews are tedious affairs, with packed agendas, vague goals, and no discipline. People pitch up reluctantly, and ill-prepared, and rely on flaky assumptions, weak excuses, and obfuscation to avoid hard decisions and accountability. Even frivolous comments can cause discussions to meander off course, and outspoken individuals are allowed too much say.

If a strategic conversation is to be effective, it must be rigorous and robust – and always respectful. Performance reviews must be the same.

Strict deadlines are always necessary, and keeping them short creates a sense of urgency. But some projects and activities will take many months or even years, so there has to be a way to sustain progress towards them.

Many firms like the notion of 100-day goals, because that seems sensibly assertive.[26] But I go further, and push clients to break all tasks into 30-day chunks, with no-holds-barred reviews at the end of each phase (Figure 3.9). This achieves five things:

1. It makes work *doable*, because people can get their arms around one small piece at a time.
2. It puts huge *pressure* into the system, thus reducing the possibility of wheelspin (which is one of the big enemies of change).
3. It lets you – and everyone else – quickly see *who* is performing, and who's not, so you can either dish out kudos or take remedial action before things get out of hand.

4. It lets you see *what* is working and what's not, in real time, so you don't have to wait for months to discover that you need to adjust your strategy.
5. It facilitates and speeds up *learning*.*

Figure 3.9

Our purpose	
Our situation	
Our challenge	
Our theory of success	
Our activities & actions	

Goals	Actions	Who	When

This approach shines a harsh light on performance, and can make people extremely uncomfortable. Some managers quickly come to dislike it, because they have to conduct reviews on schedule every month – and they have to be uncompromising about them. They have to insist on participation, exercise a firm hand in dealing with what comes up, and hold people to account for results. If

* Strategy is not a paint-by-numbers process. The point of this figure is not to suggest another form to fill in, but rather to show how your strategic conversation needs to link your purpose to your actions.

they let anyone off the hook for non-delivery, things will rapidly come unstuck.

Every review is an occasion not only to look back in order to learn, but also to look ahead and decide what's next. Each one sets things up for the 30 days ahead. So again, the tone of your conversation matters as much as the content.

If people arrive expecting to be berated and insulted, they'll be unlikely to give of their best. If, on the other hand, they find themselves in a demanding but positive environment, they'll be more constructive. They'll soon realize that these sessions are necessary and useful to the organization, and help them personally too.

This process accords perfectly with a massive shift in *personal* performance management by major firms across the world. The new approach has them dumping their traditional annual performance reviews in favour of less formal discussions that not only give employees faster and more frequent feedback, but, more importantly, help them *look ahead* to what they need to do next for both the business and themselves.

The emphasis is on growth.

This is growth leadership in action. This is strategy orchestration in action.[27]

So think about this:

By using 30-day strategy reviews well at a team level, you get to kill two birds with one stone. In the "public" process of assessing business results, you also have the ideal opportunity to praise and coach individuals – and the presence of their peers gives these conversations special weight. You'll still need to spend one-on-one time with them, and with other people who are not in the room, but these sessions are invaluable.

Disciplined execution is the eighth critical strategy practice, but this doesn't mean that it's last in a strict chain of activities, or should be the last one to get attention. For although it does depend on each of the others, they also depend on it. So, like culture, it is both a consequence and a catalyst.

Fast-cycle strategy brings clear advantages. The ability to turn your goals into action faster than your competitors – and to learn and adapt faster than they do – is the most important of these.

4

A WAY OF WORKING

The principles and practices you've just read about may sound obvious. Doesn't *everybody* know all this? Doesn't *every* company do it?

On both counts, the answer is a resounding no.

If someone asked you to explain your firm's management approach, would you immediately mention the ten essential principles or the eight critical practices? Would you be able to say you apply them all, and do it well? Not likely. And this despite the massive amount of evidence that confirms their necessity and their value.

But nor would most other CEOs have a better story to tell. And that's why, as I said in the Preface, the way is open for you to gain the advantage you want more easily than you think.

You might worry that I've said too little about the principles and practices. That each is a huge topic, deserving of far more explanation. But as I've said, my intention is to cut to the chase and get you moving.

The executives I interact with are mostly very smart people. My aim has never been to do their work for them, but rather to be a catalyst for them to do it more effectively themselves.

In a programme on case-study teaching at Harvard Business School, I learned the value of the "Zeigarnik effect," which essentially says that people remember more from unfinished or interrupted tasks or explanations than from those that are complete.*

So I've stopped where you need to start.

---

* It was first described by Lithuanian-born psychologist Bluma Zeigarnik in 1921.

The ten principles provide a context in which the eight practices help you frame your point of view about how to compete and win. Altogether, this adds up to *a way of working* that will get you the results you want. But this is just the start.

Success will be most likely if you commit to this complete approach, then stick with it and make it a way of life in your firm. And whatever else you do, it must fit with these principles and practices, complement them, and support them. If you don't take this seriously, your people won't either.

After you get going, don't let your initial enthusiasm fade and die. Remind yourself that when you introduce any new management idea, your people are alert for any sign that you're not convinced about it or committed to it for the long haul. If you falter, you'll put your credibility at risk. You'll raise the level of distrust and cynicism, and reinforce the "BOHICA effect" ("Bend over, here it comes again!") that lurks in every organization.

Of course, all firms have many other things to do. As Russell Ackoff famously said: "Managers don't solve simple, isolated problems; they manage messes."[1] A host of issues clutter their agendas, weigh them down, and distract them, so the critical core won't always be top of mind for them.

Some firms will apparently prefer other recipes, yet still succeed. Not every company will apply all of these practices in precisely the way I describe, or apply them all well. And if you asked managers in winning companies about the secrets of their success, it's quite likely that few of them would immediately cite these practices. However, if you dug deeper, you'd find this is exactly what the best performers do. So if they do this *implicitly*, imagine how much better off they would be if they were *explicit* about it.

Of course, even if you do go with the tried and true, you may not get the results you want. Many factors affect business performance. With the best will in the world, things won't always go your way. So, echoing Tom Peters, when he commented on the eight principles in *In Search of Excellence*, I offer no guarantee that if you apply these eight practices you'll make your company a winner.[2]

But here's the difference. Whereas you might have some latitude with the *Excellence* prescriptions, you have none with these. Whereas you may get away with being less than 100 per cent committed to any of those, you don't have the same liberty here.

But what if every firm *were* to apply these practices? What if you and your competitors all did the same things – one by one, and in combination? Wouldn't that level the playing field and kill anyone's competitive advantage?

To some extent, it would – and it's likely to happen because there are few secrets in business today. But there's almost no possibility that everyone would tackle all the practices in the same way, and equally well. The bigger risk is that you slow your own progress and blunt your own edge through your *inattention* to these basics, while competitors excel in them. That you keep searching for silver bullets when you already have what you need.

I'd like to have found sexier titles for these practices, for that's the way management writers seem to hook their readers. But there was no need. The practices are what they are.

Where to from here?

By now, you must be wondering: Should you bother looking for new ways to manage?

My answer: Of course you should.

Innovation in management tools and techniques is as worthy a goal as innovation in processes, products, or services. If you can find new and unique ways to run your business, you may just turbocharge your competitiveness. So stay alert to other ideas, learn all you can about them, and evaluate them within the context of the eight critical strategy practices. But if ever you think there's a case to try them, be cautious about dumping any of the practices to make way for them.

As a rule of thumb, begin with what is known to produce results, and aim to do it brilliantly. You'll make a bigger difference faster by getting the basics right than by trying to reach the moon with a sputtering organization. Not getting the basics right will ensure you don't get far.

Before you disrupt the way you work with new ideas – and you will disrupt it – be clear about what you expect to achieve. Why the need? Why now? Are you perhaps already applying methods that are best practice, but just not getting what you should from them? (And are they really *best* practice, or just fads of the moment?) Might you be better off starting from scratch and trying to discover or develop some completely new approach? And if you did do something new, what else might you sensibly *stop* doing?

Maybe you do need to radically change the way you do business. But if your firm is like so many others, that radical change may be less about experimenting with the latest ideas about management than about actually *using* familiar ones.

Slow down, act fast

A lot of clever people have been trying hard for a very long time to make their firms more competitive. This is a never-ending quest, and for reasons I've explained, most find it both daunting and frustrating. They almost always underestimate just how hard it is and how long it will take to change their ways.

As Frederick Taylor pointed out, "If anyone expects large results in six months or a year in a large works he is looking for the impossible."[3] Eiji Toyoda, scion of the family that founded Toyota, and his production head, Taiichi Ohno, took 20 years to fully apply the ideas that became the Toyota Production System. They arrived at most of the principles of lean production by the early 1960s, and the firm has been relentlessly using them and fine-tuning them ever since – for 50-some years.[4] The renowned leadership skills of General Electric have been honed over more than a century. Apple, Nestlé, Amazon, and Boeing have been decades in the making.

Some of the changes you want to make will doubtless take a long time. Others can be made in next to no time. So it makes sense to *slow down* in thinking things through and deciding what to do, and then to *act fast.*

None of what I've suggested needs to be chewed to death. Nor should you see complexity in it that doesn't exist. The eight critical strategy practices make playing to win as simple as it can be. But when all is said and done, their value lies entirely in *how you use them to talk your way through the challenges to come.*

And that you can start doing right now.

Choose your commitments with care

My many years of experience as a consultant have taught me that managers are highly unlikely to stick with what they say in strategy meetings. No matter how definite they seem at the time, they'll soon be busy with something else.

This happens because things change and they have to adapt. But it also happens because they simply change their minds.

Many of their "commitments" – whether to a strategy, a practice, or an action – turn out to be hot air. They say what sounds right for a particular moment, but haven't really thought it through, and may not really mean it either. Then, real-world events overtake them, making even their best intentions inappropriate.

Another reality is that they don't clear the decks for new initiatives. Instead, they just load their latest ideas onto work already in the system. This clogs the corporate arteries and confuses everyone.

And, as if they need more reasons to fail, they also flit from one management idea to another, often trying to use concepts they don't understand and don't know how to apply.

A lack of commitment and staying power is normal, not an aberration. It shows up in many ways.

You see it when managers talk in their vision statements about being "world class," but then won't do what it takes to get there. When they proclaim the need to be a "low-cost supplier," but won't make the hard decisions required to get their costs down. When they say, "Customer service is our competitive advantage," but then stay as far away from customers as they can. When they say, "People are our most valuable resource," but then act in ways that show they don't really mean it. When they boast about being "disruptors," but won't invest in innovation or take risks with their current business. Or when they insist on planning in great detail for the next five or ten years, but then quickly get knocked off course by unexpected events, or second-guess themselves for no good reason.

Incentives muddy the waters too. Managers make a hoo-hah about a particular process, but track and reward performance in others. They say, "We have to be passionate about customers," but then dish out bonuses based solely on profit growth. Or they trumpet the need for innovation, but celebrate and reward cost-cutting. And their actions blot out their words.

Commitment – whether to a strategy, a practice, a project, or a set of values – is critical to business success. But staying committed is extremely hard. No two days are the same. There are many distractions. There's always something more interesting or urgent to do. And sudden winds blow companies this way and that.

In summary

1. **Don't allow your search for new ways to manage to distract you from attending to the basics of your business.** You may get bored doing this, but fight the feeling. If you err on the fundamentals, no amount of management novelty will save your bacon.
2. **Don't confuse a *style* of management with fundamental *ideas about* management.** The way you manage, and the theories you use, are related but different.
3. **Don't dump proven practices too quickly.** It is very tempting to keep trying new ideas. Some may have immense value. But changing almost anything is more disruptive, distracting, difficult, and time-consuming than anyone expects. There are always hidden costs and unintended consequences. And in any case, we have a pretty good idea of what works, so perhaps you should simply start doing it. Or maybe intensify your efforts.
4. **Before you adopt any new management idea, check its soundness.** Who produced it? What assumptions is it based on? What evidence supports it? Where else and under what circumstances has it worked? Why might it be good for you – and can

you make it work? If you don't do your homework, you're looking for trouble.

5. **Think through how you'll make the switch from one management practice to another.** You may believe that introducing new ideas will make you look like a visionary, and give your business a lift. And maybe it will. But beware of throwing the baby out with the bathwater. New ideas are inherently risky – and, as we have seen, in short supply – so best you introduce them cautiously, and test them carefully.
6. **Consider how you'll integrate your new approach into your current business model.** It's easy to foul up the works. To assume that any new idea will "plug and play" is to play with fire; most don't. Because an organization is a complex system, a seemingly minor change can have ripple effects that cause trouble in unexpected places. Some of your people will resist what you do, or be unable to adapt to new ways. New processes may not sit well with old ones, and information systems might not talk to each other. Customers and suppliers may baulk if you suddenly expect them to act differently. For these reasons, and others, it's important to (a) take a holistic view of things before you start tweaking, and (b) think carefully about *how* you'll make changes.
7. **Allow for change to be harder than you think, and to take longer and cost more.** Most change efforts fail. Delivery dates are missed. Budgets are overshot. Outcomes are off beam. You might imagine that you can do things differently, but don't bank on it. Be ambitious, by all means, but be realistic too. Stretch goals and tight deadlines are essential in getting things done, but unreasonable expectations can set your team up to fail.

And above all,

8. **Travel light and don't keep adding to your already heavy workload.** Keep things simple and make the eight critical strategy practices a way of life. They are the critical core.

We've come full circle. I promised you a simple, sound, and practical approach to business leadership which is based on just one tool – *strategic conversation* – and centred on two words: *strategy* and *people.*

The Critical Core describes that approach, and will help you make it a way of life in your company.

I've focused on *what* you need to do more than *how* you might do it, because you have no latitude with the what, but virtually unlimited choices about the how. The first is mandatory. The second is entirely up to you. Without the critical strategy practices as your guide, and without constant vigilance against a tsunami of recycled, overhyped, and redundant management tools, you will not have enough hours in the day to do what you should be doing – which is, basically, to make and sell things or provide services.

I've also shown that applying the practices doesn't have to be complicated. Each of them rests on a few simple questions, and together they form the core of your strategic conversation. How you craft and conduct that conversation is what sets you apart in the market.

This is simple stuff.

You don't need more complicated answers.

The critical core makes your difference a reality.

The Critical Core tells you how to make it reality.

APPENDIX

WHAT POPULAR STUDIES TELL US

Producing checklists for success is the stock-in-trade of management experts. Here are some famous examples – nine books and two articles. Each offers its own take on management, and there's merit in all of them. Not surprisingly, for reasons I've spelled out, there's little here that's particularly remarkable or innovative, and there are many similarities and some overlap. Unfortunately, none of this guarantees anything.

BOOKS

In Search of Excellence by Thomas J. Peters and Robert H. Waterman (New York: Harper & Row, 1982)

1. A bias for action
2. Close to the customer
3. Autonomy and entrepreneurship
4. Productivity through people
5. Hands-on, value-driven
6. Stick to the knitting
7. Simple form, lean staff
8. Simultaneous loose-tight properties

Vanguard Management by James O'Toole (New York: Doubleday, 1985)

James O'Toole was of the view that "the best way to deal with a subjective issue is to ask a subjective question." So he asked some 200 people, "If you could choose to work in any *large* American corporation, which one would it be?" Most cited at least one of the following eight companies: Atlantic Richfield, Control Data, Dayton-Hudson, Deere, Honeywell, Levi Strauss, Motorola, and Weyerhauser.

With the help of 60 graduate students of his, O'Toole then looked for reasons why these "Vanguard companies" stood out, and came up with a list of seven characteristics (Figure A).

He also produced a list of eight "Old Guard" behaviours, arguing that corporations practising one or more of these "almost always fail."

Figure A

The Vanguard	The Old Guard
1. People-oriented	1. Insensitive to the realities of the external environment
2. Leaders are visible	2. Diversify out of their expertise and thus lose sight of the basics
3. Plan for employment stability	3. Make facile assumptions about the future
4. Have a consumer orientation	4. Become smug and complacent
5. Future-oriented	5. Become overly action-oriented and insufficiently thoughtful
6. Provide a sense of ownership	6. Repeat past successes and ignore the need for change
7. Are a link with entrepreneurial small businesses	7. Think short-term
	8. Behave as if the only purpose of a corporation is to maximize shareholder wealth

Built to Last by James C. Collins and Jerry I. Porras (New York: HarperBusiness, 1994)

1. Clock building, not time telling
2. No "tyranny of the OR"
3. More than profits
4. Preserve the core/stimulate progress
5. Big hairy audacious goals
6. Cult-like cultures
7. Try a lot of stuff and see what works
8. Home-grown management
9. Good enough never is

The Discipline of Market Leaders by Michael Treacy and Fred Wiersema (New York: Addison-Wesley, 1995)

1. Operational excellence
2. Customer intimacy
3. Product leadership

Good to Great by Jim Collins (New York: HarperBusiness, 2001)

1. Level 5 leadership
2. First who ... then what
3. Confront the brutal facts
4. The hedgehog concept
5. A culture of discipline
6. Technology accelerators
7. The flywheel and the doom loop

The Agenda by Michael Hammer (New York: Random House, 2001)

1. Run your business for your customers
2. Give your customers what they really want
3. Put processes first
4. Create order where chaos reigns
5. Measure like you mean it
6. Manage without structure
7. Focus on the final customer
8. Knock down your outer walls
9. Extend your enterprise

What Really Works by William Joyce, Nitin Nohria, and Bruce Roberson (New York: HarperBusiness, 2003)

Primary

1. Make your strategy clear and focused
2. Develop and maintain flawless operational execution
3. Develop and maintain a performance-based culture
4. Build and maintain a fast, flexible, flat organization

Secondary

1. Hold onto talented employees and find more
2. Keep leaders and directors committed to the business
3. Make innovations that are industry transforming
4. Make growth happen with mergers and partnerships

Great by Choice by Jim Collins and Morten Hansen (New York: HarperBusiness, 2011)

1. 10X leadership
2. 20-mile march

3. Fire bullets, then cannonballs
4. Leading above the death line
5. SMaC
6. Return on luck

Staying Power by Michael A. Cusumano (Oxford: Oxford University Press, 2010)

1. Platforms, not just products
2. Services, not just products (or platforms)
3. Capabilities, not just strategy
4. Pull, don't just push
5. Flexibility, not just efficiency

ARTICLES

"The Four Principles of Enduring Success" by Christian Stadler (*Harvard Business Review*, July–August 2007)

1. Exploit before you explore
2. Diversify your business portfolio
3. Remember your mistakes
4. Be conservative about change

"Three Rules for Making a Company Truly Great" by Michael E. Raynor and Mumtaz Ahmed (*Harvard Business Review*, April 2013)

1. Better before cheaper – in other words, compete on differentiators other than price
2. Revenue before cost – that is, prioritize increasing revenue over reducing costs
3. There are no other rules – so change anything you must to follow Rules 1 and 2

NOTES

INTRODUCTION: WHY THIS BOOK?

1. "Russell Ackoff – Systems-Based Improvement," http://www.youtube.com/watch?v=_pcuzRq-rDU
2. Peter F. Drucker, *The Practice of Management*, New York: Harper & Row, 1954

CHAPTER 1: GETTING TO THE CORE

1. Andrew S. Grove, *Only the Paranoid Survive*, New York: Doubleday, 1996
2. Mary Yoko Brannen and Yves Doz, "Corporate Languages and Strategic Agility," *California Management Review*, Vol. 54, No. 3, Spring 2012
3. Edgar Schein, "SMR Forum: Does Japanese Management Style Have a Message for American Managers?" *Sloan Management Review*, Fall 1981
4. Max H. Bazerman and Michael D. Watkins, *Predictable Surprises*, Boston: Harvard Business School Press, 2004
5. Thomas J. Peters and Robert H. Waterman, *In Search of Excellence*, New York: Harper & Row, 1982
6. James C. Collins and Jerry I. Porras, *Built to Last*, New York: HarperBusiness, 1994
7. Michael Treacy and Fred Wiersema, *The Discipline of Market Leaders*, New York: Addison-Wesley, 1995
8. Jim Collins, *Good to Great*, New York: HarperBusiness, 2001
9. Jim Collins, *Great by Choice*, New York: HarperBusiness, 2011
10. Michael A. Cusumano, *Staying Power*, New York: Oxford University Press, 2010
11. William Joyce, Nitin Nohria, and Bruce Roberson, *What Really Works*, New York: HarperBusiness, 2003
12. James O'Toole, *Vanguard Management*, New York: Doubleday, 1985
13. Michael Hammer, *The Agenda*, New York: Random House, 2001

14. Christian Stadler, "The Four Principles of Enduring Success," *Harvard Business Review*, July–August 2007
15. Michael E. Raynor and Mumtaz Ahmed, "Three Rules for Making a Company Truly Great," *Harvard Business Review*, April 2013
16. John J. Tarrant, *Drucker: The Man Who Invented Corporate Society*, New York: Cahners Books, 1976
17. Dorothy Leonard and Walter Swap, *Deep Smarts*, Boston: Harvard Business School Press, 2005
18. John Gardner, *Changing Minds*, Boston: Harvard Business School Press, 2004
19. Peter F. Drucker, "Thinking Ahead: Potentials of Management Science," *Harvard Business Review*, January–February 1959

CHAPTER 2: ESSENTIAL PRINCIPLES

1. Peter F. Drucker, *The Practice of Management*, New York: Harper & Row, 1954; Pankaj Ghemawat, *Commitment: The Dynamic of Strategy*, New York: The Free Press, 1991; Michael E. Porter, "What Is Strategy?" *Harvard Business Review*, November–December 1996
2. Scott E. Page, "Path Dependence," *Quarterly Journal of Political Science*, Vol. 1, 2006
3. Karl E. Weick, *Sensemaking in Organizations*, Thousand Oaks, California: Sage Publications, 1995; Karl E. Weick and Kathleen M. Sutcliffe, *Managing the Unexpected*, San Francisco: Jossey-Bass, 2001; Richard Normann, *Reframing Business*, Chichester: John Wiley & Sons, 2001; Sarah Kaplan and Paula Jarzabkowski, "Using Strategy Tools in Practice – How Tools Mediate Strategizing and Organizing," Advanced Institute of Management Research, Paper No. 047, August 2006; James March, *The Ambiguities of Experience*, New York: Cornell University Press, 2010; Sarah Kaplan, "Strategy and Powerpoint," *Organization Science*, Vol. 22, No. 2, 2011; Sarah Kaplan and Wanda J. Orlikowski, "Temporal Work in Strategy Making," *Organization Science*, Vol. 24, No. 4, 2013; J.P. Eggers and Sarah Kaplan, "Cognition and Capabilities," *The Academy of Management Annals*, Vol. 7, No. 1, May 2013
4. Chester I. Barnard, *The Functions of the Executive*, Cambridge, Massachusetts: Harvard University Press, 1938
5. Richard Rumelt, *Good Strategy, Bad Strategy*, New York: Crown Business, 2011
6. Ibid.

7. Gary Hamel and C.K. Prahalad, "Strategic Intent," *Harvard Business Review*, May–June 1989
8. Christopher A. Bartlett and Sumantra Ghoshal, "Changing the Role of Top Management: Beyond Strategy to Purpose," *Harvard Business Review*, November 1994; Tony Manning, *Making Sense of Strategy*, Cape Town: Zebra Press, 2001; Rick Warren, *The Purpose-Driven Life*, Grand Rapids, Michigan: Zondervan, 2002; Nikos Mourkogiannis, *Purpose*, New York: Palgrave Macmillan, 2006
9. Tony Manning, *Making Sense of Strategy*, Cape Town: Zebra Press, 2001
10. "Quick and Dirty," *The Economist*, 8–14 October 2016
11. Robert Simons, "The Business of Business Schools: Restoring a Focus on Competing to Win," *Capitalism and Society*, Vol. 8, No. 1, 2013
12. "Jack Welch Cracks the Whip Again," *Business Week*, 14 December 1997
13. Francesco Guerrera, "Welch Condemns Share Price Focus," *Financial Times*, 12 March 2009
14. Michael E. Porter and Mark R. Kramer, "Strategy and Society," *Harvard Business Review*, December 2006
15. Michael E. Porter and Mark R. Kramer, "Creating Shared Value," *Harvard Business Review*, January–February 2011
16. Martin Neil Baily and Frank Comes, "Prospects for Growth: An Interview with Robert Solow," *McKinsey Quarterly*, September 2014
17. Louis V. Gerstner, *Who Says Elephants Can't Dance?* New York: HarperCollins, 2002
18. Richard A. D'Aveni, *Beating the Commodity Trap*, Boston: Harvard Business Press, 2010
19. "Historically Speaking: A Roundtable with Alfred D. Chandler, Nancy F. Koehn, Debora L. Spar, and Richard S. Tedlow," *Leading Research*, Harvard Business School, http://www.leadingresearch.hbs.edu/story02.html, accessed 4 April 2008
20. Charles A. O'Reilly III and Michael L. Tushman, "Organizational Ambidexterity: Past, Present and Future," Research Paper No. 2130, Stanford Graduate School of Business, June 2013
21. Kenneth R. Andrews, *The Concept of Corporate Strategy*, Homewood, Illinois: Richard D. Irwin Inc., 1980
22. Michael E. Porter, "What Is Strategy?" *Harvard Business Review*, November–December 1996
23. Martin Neil Baily and Frank Comes, "Prospects for Growth: An Interview with Robert Solow," *McKinsey Quarterly*, September 2014

24. Fred Gluck, Michael G. Jacobides, and Dan Simpson, "Synthesis, Capabilities, and Overlooked Insights: Next Frontiers for Strategists," *McKinsey Quarterly*, September 2014
25. Richard Rumelt, *Good Strategy, Bad Strategy*, New York: Crown Business, 2011
26. Michael E. Porter, "CEO as Strategist," *Leadership Excellence*, September 2005
27. Eric Van den Steen, "A Theory of Explicitly Formulated Strategy," Working Paper 12-102, Harvard Business School, May 2012
28. Thomas J. Peters and Robert H. Waterman, *In Search of Excellence*, New York: Harper & Row, 1982
29. Henry Mintzberg, Bruce Ahlstrand, and Joseph Lampel, *Strategy Safari*, New York: The Free Press, 1990
30. Kurt Lewin, "Frontiers in Group Dynamics," in D. Cartwright, editor, *Field Theory in Social Science*, London: Social Science Paperbacks, 1952; Richard Beckhard and Reuben T. Harris, *Organizational Transitions*, New York: Addison-Wesley, 1987; W. Warner Burke, *Organization Development*, New York: Addison-Wesley, 1987
31. Abraham Zaleznick, "Managers and Leaders: Are They Different?" *Harvard Business Review*, March–April 1977; John P. Kotter, "What Leaders Really Do," *Harvard Business Review*, March 1990; John Kotter, *John Kotter on What Leaders Really Do*, Boston: Harvard Business School Press, 1999
32. Henry Mintzberg, *Managers Not MBAs*, San Francisco: Berrett-Koehler Publishers, 2004; Cynthia A. Montgomery, *The Strategist*, New York: HarperBusiness, 2012
33. Sarah Kaplan and Paula Jarzabkowski, "Using Strategy Tools In Practice – How Tools Mediate Strategizing and Organizing," Advanced Institute of Management Research, Paper No. 047, August 2006
34. Scott E. Page, "Path Dependence," *Quarterly Journal of Political Science*, Vol. 1, 2006
35. Interview with the author, 2004
36. Dorothy Leonard and Walter Swap, *Deep Smarts*, Boston: Harvard Business School Press, 2005; K. Anders Ericksson, Neil Charness, Paul J. Feltovich, and Robert R. Hoffman, editors, *The Cambridge Handbook of Expertise and Expert Performance*, Cambridge: Cambridge University Press, 2006; Malcolm Gladwell, *Outliers*, New York: Little, Brown and Company, 2008; Eugen Herrigel, *Zen in the Art of Archery*, London:

Routledge & Kegan Paul, 1953; Steven J. Spear, "Learning to Lead at Toyota," *Harvard Business Review*, May 2004

37. Gerd Gigerenzer, *Gut Feelings*, New York: Viking Penguin, 2007

CHAPTER 3: THE CRITICAL PRACTICES

1. Peter F. Drucker, "Thinking Ahead: Potentials of Management Science," *Harvard Business Review*, January–February 1959
2. John P. Kotter, "What Leaders Really Do," *Harvard Business Review*, May–June 1990
3. Stephen R. Covey, *The 7 Habits of Highly Successful People*, New York: Simon & Schuster, 1989
4. John P. Kotter, *The New Rules*, New York: The Free Press, 1995
5. Henry Mintzberg, *Managing*, San Francisco: Berrett-Koehler Publishers, 2009
6. Jay Lorsch, "A Contingency Theory of Leadership," *Handbook of Leadership Theory and Practice*, edited by Nitin Nohria and Rakesh Khurana, Boston: Harvard Business Press, 2010
7. Malcolm S. Knowles, *The Modern Practice of Adult Education*, Cambridge: The Adult Education Company, 1980
8. William A. Sherden, *The Fortune Sellers*, New York: John Wiley, 1998
9. Peter Cornelius, Alexander Van de Putte, and Mattia Romani, "Three Decades of Scenario Planning at Shell," *California Management Review*, Vol. 48, No. 1, Fall 2005
10. Nate Silver, *The Signal and the Noise*, New York: Allen Lane, 2012
11. Ben Lauderdale, "What We Got Wrong in Our 2015 U.K. General Election Model," 8 May 2015, fivethirtyeight.com
12. Nassim Nicholas Taleb, *The Black Swan*, New York: Random House, 2007
13. Tim Harford, *Adapt*, London: Little, Brown and Company, 2011
14. George Stalk Jr, "Time – the Next Source of Competitive Advantage," *Harvard Business Review*, July–August 1988; Tony Manning, *The Race to Learn*, Cape Town: Juta & Co., 1991; Yves Doz and Mikko Kosonen, *Fast Strategy*, London: Pearson Education, 2008; Steven J. Spear, *The High-Velocity Edge*, New York: McGraw-Hill, 2009; Jocelyn R. Davis, Henry M. Frechette Jr, and Edwin H. Boswell, *Strategic Speed*, Boston: Harvard Business Press, 2010
15. Sumantra Ghoshal and Christopher A. Bartlett, "Changing the Role of Top Management: Beyond Strategy to Purpose," *Harvard Business*

Review, November–December 1994; Sumantra Ghoshal and Christopher A. Bartlett, "Changing the Role of Top Management: Beyond Structure to Processes," *Harvard Business Review*, January–February 1995; Sumantra Ghoshal and Christopher A. Bartlett, "Changing the Role of Top Management: Beyond Systems to People," *Harvard Business Review*, May–June 1995

16. Tony Manning, "A New Model for Strategists," *Tony Manning's Strategy Letter*, Issue No. 9, July 1994
17. Tony Manning, "Beyond Strategy to Purpose," *Tony Manning's Strategy Letter*, Issue No. 12, April 1995
18. Hiroyuki Itami, *Mobilizing Invisible Assets*, Cambridge, Massachusetts: Harvard University Press, 1987
19. David J. Collis and Cynthia A. Montgomery, "Competing on Resources," *Harvard Business Review*, July 2008
20. Donald N. Sull, *Revival of the Fittest*, Boston: Harvard Business School Press, 2003
21. Liisa Välikangas, *The Resilient Organization*, New York: McGraw-Hill, 2010
22. Steven P. Schnaars, *Managing Imitation Strategies*, New York: The Free Press, 1994; Paul Geroski, *Fast Second*, San Francisco: Jossey-Bass, 2004
23. Mehrdad Baghai, Stephen C. Coley, and David White with Charles Conn and Robert J. McLean, "Staircases to Growth," *McKinsey Quarterly*, November 1996; Mehrdad Baghai, Stephen Coley, and David White, *The Alchemy of Growth*, New York: Perseus Publishing, 1999
24. Lawrence G. Hrebiniak, *Making Strategy Work*, Upper Saddle River, New Jersey: Wharton School Publishing, 2005; Michael C. Mankins and Richard Steele, "Turning Great Strategy into Great Performance," *Harvard Business Review*, July 2005; Donald Sull, Rebecca Homkes, and Charles Sull, "Why Strategy Execution Unravels – and What to Do About It," *Harvard Business Review*, March 2015
25. Mark Morgan, Raymond E. Levitt, and William Malek, *Executing Your Strategy*, Boston: Harvard Business School Press, 2007
26. Paddy Miller, *Mission Critical*, Maidenhead: McGraw-Hill, 2001
27. Peter Cappelli and Anna Tavis, "The Performance Management Revolution," *Harvard Business Review*, October 2016

CHAPTER 4: A WAY OF WORKING

1. Ian I. Mitroff, Can M. Alpaslan, and Richard O. Mason, "The Messy Business of Management," *Sloan Management Review*, Vol. 54, No. 1, Fall 2012
2. Tom Peters, "Tom Peters's True Confessions," *Fast Company*, Issue 53, November 2001
3. Frederick W. Taylor, "Shop Management," lecture to meeting of mechanical engineers held at the United States Hotel, Saratoga, New York, June 1903
4. James P. Womack, Daniel T. Jones, and Daniel Roos, *The Machine That Changed the World*, New York: Rawson Associates, 1990

By the same author

What's Wrong With Management and How to Get It Right

What winning companies do that puts them ahead in the race for customers and profits

In today's rapidly changing and increasingly complex world, companies everywhere struggle to meet new challenges and continue to underperform – and despite churning out a constant stream of theories and tools, the management ideas industry has made little progress in advancing management thought.

In this provocative book, top strategy consultant Tony Manning brings managers the insights and advice they need for the coming decades of turbulence and hypercompetition.

Drawing lessons from 100 years of management history, plus his own extensive research and experience, he shows how management's frenetic quest for "silver bullets" has led to confusion and complexity rather than clarity and simplicity. And he identifies eight critical strategy practices that apply to every company everywhere, and explains how to use them.

This fascinating and practical guide is a must-read for anyone interested in improving business results.

ISBN 978 1 77022 899 3 (print)
ISBN 978 1 77022 900 6 (ePub)
ISBN 978 1 77022 901 3 (PDF)